150 MORE STORIES

for
PREACHERS
and
TEACHERS

Jack McArdle

TWENTY-THIRD PUBLICATIONS
Mystic, Connecticut 06355

Design by Bill Bolger

Origination by The Columba Press
93 The Rise, Mount Merrion, Blackrock, Co Dublin, Ireland

Third printing 1996

Twenty-Third Publications
185 Willow Street
P.O. Box 180
Mystic, CT 06355
(860) 536-2611
800-321-0411

© Copyright 1993 Jack McArdle, ss cc.   All rights reserved.
No part of this publication may be reproduced in any manner
without prior written permission of the publisher. Write to
Permissions Editor.

ISBN 0-89622-540-2
Library of Congress Catalog Card Number 92-82675
Printed in the U.S.A

Contents

"Someone on the wit side of wisdom said, 'Humans were created because God likes stories.' If this is so, God must like Jack McArdle very much. His stories are delightful, pithy, and to the point; and, just in case we miss the point of a story, 2 or 3 more points are suggested at the end of each. Some of these morals are sure-fire 'gotchas': a message that 'gets you thinking.'

"It is written for preachers and teachers and also for random readers. There's enough stories to make the book a joy, and enough 'gotchas' to make it a good tool for an examination of conscience."

Rev. Isaias Powers, C.P.
Author, *Women of the Gospel: Sharing God's Compassion*

"Recently Cardinal Roger Mahoney of Los Angeles wrote, 'For thousands of years, people have told stories whenever they were frightened, lonely or confused and needed to gather together to make sense of their lives...stories of love and stories of war, stories of courage and stories of despair, factual stories and made-up ones....Stories delight us. We love to tell them, and we love to listen to them. Why? Because we are storytellers.'

"Indeed we are. As indeed Jesus was. Therefore preachers and teachers always do well to tap this fundamental human proclivity. And that is why we are always grateful for collections such as Rev. Jack McArdle has gathered in this book. It's a rich mine of wisdom, resource and inspiration to flesh out the living scriptural word."

Rev. William Bausch
Author, *Storytelling, Imagination and Faith*

"A collection of stories that will help parents, teachers, and preachers even more than 150 times to find a story they need to help them make a point. Invaluable."

Rev. Joseph Donders, M.Afr.
Author, *Empowering Hope: Stories to Brighten Your Day*

Thematic Index

Introduction

This is a second collection of stories and anecdotes to help the preacher and the teacher. It differs from the first collection in this significant way: I have added after each story some possible conclusions, teachings, or points for reflection. These are deliberately little more than hints. Their purpose is to suggest how a story or incident might be used to help make a point more graphic or memorable.

The lessons to be drawn from many of the stories are self-evident. The stories are not intended to amuse or entertain. As Msgr. McGarry, a former teacher of homiletics, used to say, "Remember that your task is to feed the sheep, not to entertain the goats." Before using a story, however, you should answer this question honestly: "Why am I going to use this story? To instruct, to convey a basic teaching, to simply to fill out my homily material and time, or just to get a laugh (not always bad)?"

I place this second collection of stories and anecdotes in your hands with trust, hope, respect, and gratitude.

May the Spirit anoint your words.

1 Look into your own heart

A young businessman began dating a charming young actress. The relationship progressed and developed until it reached the point when the businessman was considering the possibility of marrying the young woman. Being a very cautious businessman, he hired a private detective to check out the young actress, to ensure there weren't any skeletons in her closet.

The detective knew nothing of the relationship; in fact, he was just given the young woman's name. He did his work very thoroughly, and finally submitted the results of his investigation. It went something like this: "This is a very charming, honest, and upright young lady. There seems to be but one blemish on her character. It appears that, of late, she has been keeping company with a young businessman of very doubtful character, and of questionable reputation."

—"*Hypocrite! First get rid of the beam out of your own eye, and then you can see the speck in your brother's eye*" (Mt 7:5).

—*When I point one finger at another, there are three fingers pointing at me.*

2 Doing what Jesus did

There was a funeral in town. Everybody would be there. The parish priest had to go elsewhere that day, but he was happy that the funeral was in the hands of an intelligent, common-sense, no-nonsense curate.

That evening, when he returned he asked the curate how the funeral had gone. "Ah, it went OK," he said. "No great problems. A huge crowd. Oh, by the way, I had one small problem." "What was that?" "Mrs Robinson was at the funeral, and as you know, she's Protestant." "Oh, that's no problem. I would have expected her to be there. A good friend of the family and all." "Oh, but she came up for Communion," said the curate. This rivoted the parish priest to his chair, as he turned with a look of horror on his face. "What happened?" he gasped. "Well," said the curate, "she was in my line for Communion. She was about two away from me when I spotted her..." "Go on, go on," said the parish priest, "what did you do? What did you do?" "Well," said the curate, "I didn't know what to do. I had to make a snap decision. I just decided right there and then that I would do what I believe Jesus would have done." "Oh my God, no!" exclaimed the parish priest, "surely you didn't do that!"

– *Jesus has always had a problem with very religious people—in fact, he was crucified by them!*

– *Religion is external obligation, performed by us and can be devoid of spirituality, which is an inside job, and is the work of the Spirit.*

3

To really care

One Sunday a priest began his homily by holding up a huge triangle. Then he said, "My homily this morning is like this triangle. It has three points...

– The first is this: Because we fail to accept, love, and forgive each other as Jesus taught us, people are starving, hurting, and being killed in today's world...

The second point is that most people don't give a damn about this...

– And the third point is that some of you listening to me now could be more concerned that I used the word 'damn' than you are about all those people who are suffering and dying."

– *When I die the questions I'll be asked will be scandalously materialistic; I'll be asked about bread, water, clothes, etc.*

– *I cannot pick and choose from the gospel. It is all or nothing.*

– *The six exam questions that will be on my finals (when I die!) are in Matthew's gospel, chapter 25.*

4 Me, an evangelist?

A young man knew that because of his baptism and confirmation he was called to proclaim the gospel. He was shy and timid, and of little education. He felt that the task was beyond him.

He thought about it over a period, then he came up with a solution for his problem. Each week he set aside a certain amount of his wages, and with this he bought simple booklets about Jesus and the message of the gospel. He placed the booklets in hospitals, railway stations, doctors' waiting rooms and other appropriate places.

One day he actually heard a new convert say, "My introduction to the church came through a booklet I picked up in the waiting room of the railway station here in town."

– *The gospel is in between two phases, "Come and See" and "Go and Tell."*

– *If I am not actively engaged in evangelizing others, chances are that I have not been evangelized myself.*

5 Made in his image

A little girl was sitting at the kitchen table with a few sheets of paper and a box of crayons. She was drawing a picture. "What are you drawing?" her mother asked her. "I'm drawing a picture of God," was the reply. "But, darling," said her mother, "nobody knows what God looks like." And the little girl replied, "But they will when I have finished the picture."

– *The image is within—the Inner Child—well hidden behind the Ego, the salesperson's basket of goodies that we carry out in front to impress those we meet.*

– *Could Ego stand for Edging God Out?*

6 When you pray

Three clergy men were discussing different prayer postures. Each was convinced that his way was the best. One man was convinced that kneeling was the correct posture in prayer. Another was equally convinced that the proper posture was to be seated cross-legged on the floor. Another said that, like Jesus, he always prayed "looking heavenward."

There was an electrician listening to the discussion. He interrupted them to tell that of all the postures he ever used in prayer, he prayed more sincerely one time than any other—that was when he was hanging upside down by one leg from a telephone pole in a thunderstorm, when his ladder slipped!

– God looks at, and listens to the heart, when we pray...

– The organ God has given me to pray with is my heart. If the heart is not praying, then the tongue is wasting its time, no matter what the body posture is!

7 Where is Jesus?

This young girl was getting married. The whole ceremony was very important to her, and she had given a great deal of thought to planning something really beautiful. She even suggested that a glass of champagne around the altar afterwards could help have the celebration begin in the proper place, and would bridge the gap between church and hotel. The curate gave the OK for this, in the knowledge that that was the parish priest's day off, and he need never know!

The crowd was gathered around the altar, glasses in hand, and the festivities were in full swing, when the parish priest arrived back unexpectedly, and came storming out of the sacristy.

On being told that the curate had given the go-ahead for this, he headed for the presbytery next door. The curate knew he was caught, but, putting on a brave face, he spoke about the wedding at Cana, and all the wine Jesus had provided for the feast. At that, the parish priest exploded, "That was totally and utterly different. The Blessed Sacrament wasn't there."

– *Jesus is most present in the worshipping community.*

– *This is a good example of a very antiseptic form of religion, which can make us so heavenly that we end up being no earthly good!*

8 Transplanted

Consider for a moment the whole concept of a heart transplant, and then see the way it can teach us truths even more profound.

The old heart, the defective heart, is removed. This had gone wrong, and is not functioning properly. Removing the defective heart is a very good way of thinking of repentance, which is a rejection of the old, a turning my back on old ways.

The second part of the process is implant. This involves placing the new heart in the body so that the whole system can begin to work properly again. This implant, or transplant, is the equivalent of new life, of rebirth, of being born again.

– *"I will take out that heart of stone and give you a heart of flesh"* (Ez 11:19).

– *"Create a new heart within me, O Lord, and put a steadfast spirit within me"* (Ps 51: 10).

– *Quite often in scripture, God's work in us is described as removing the old and replacing it with the new: "Behold I make all things new" (Is 65:17). "I will give them a new heart and mind" (Ez 11:19).*

– *"A new creation in Jesus Christ is not just the old man patched up, but an altogether new person living in the same body" (Peter Marshall).*

9 Supplying the material

A rich man had a dream in which he died and went to heaven. St Peter escorted him down a lovely street on which each house was magnificent. The rich man saw one house that was particularly beautiful. "That," said Peter, "is the house of one of your servants."

"Well," said the man, smiling, "if my servant has a building like that, then I'm really looking forward to seeing my own magnificent mansion."

Soon they came to a very small street where the houses were tiny. "You will live in that hut," said St Peter, pointing his finger. "Me, live in that hovel!" roared the man in great anger. "This is the best we can do for you," explained St Peter. "You must understand that we only build your home up here with the material you send ahead while you are still on earth."

– God won't send you anywhere when you die—to hell or to heaven. He will eternalize whatever direction you are traveling in now.

– Heaven really begins down here on earth.

10 Preaching the Bible

A chaplain on a battlefield came across a young man who was lying in a shell hole, seriously wounded. "Would you like me to read you something from this book, the Bible?" he asked. "I'm so thirsty; I'd rather have a drink of water," the soldier said. Hurrying away, the chaplain soon brought the water. Then the wounded man said, "Could you put something under my head?'

The chaplain took off his overcoat, rolled it up, and gently placed it under the man's head for a pillow. "Now," said the suffering man, "if I just had something over me—I'm cold."

The chaplain immediately removed his jacket and put it over the wounded man to keep him warm. Then the soldier looked the chaplain straight in the eye and said, "If there's anything in that book that makes a man do for another all that you have done for me, then please read it, because I'd love to hear it."

– *If my actions don't speak of gospel values, be sure my words never will.*

– *What affects people most is often caught rather than taught.*

11 God's plan for us

Once upon a time three young trees were growing side by side in a huge plantation. With typical youthful enthusiasm, they shared with one another their hopes for life when they reached maturity.

One hoped to be used in the building of some mansion, so that its grain and quality would be admired by the great and the famous.

The second hoped to form the tallest mast in the most beautiful sailing ship, thus gaining full attention as it sailed into any port.

The third hoped to be part of some big public spectacle, well out in the open, so that passers-by would stop and look on in wonder.

The reality for the trees, according to the legend, was:
– the first was cut down, and part of it was used to make a trough for animals, and it later became a manger in a stable.
– the second was cut down, and part of it was used to make a very simple fishing boat that spent a lot of its time tied up on the shores of the Sea of Galilee.
– the third was cut down, and part of it was used to form the beams of a cross, which was used for crucifixion.

– *Despite the dreams of each individual tree, God had a personal plan and purpose for each.*

– *The ideal is to be available for God to use me in any way he chooses to establish, to promote, and to build up the kingdom of his Son Jesus Christ.*

12 Mopping up

The phrase "mopping up" was used by soldiers in World War II. For example, an island in the Pacific is liberated by the American military forces. However, there were always pockets of resistance holding up in the jungles, either because they were unaware of what had happened or they stubbornly refused to surrender.

"Mopping up" was simply a case of tidying up the loose ends, of firmly establishing and consolidating a victory already achieved. The real battle had already been fought and victory was already assured.

– A very good example of our work as Christians: mopping up! Jesus already has achieved the victory. It is up to us to face up to any remaining resistance we encounter within ourselves.

– "Lord, by your cross and resurrection, you have set us free. You are the Savior of the World."

– "Dying, you destroyed our death; rising you restored our life."

– When we speak of Jesus we use the past tense—his work is done. Now it's up to us to do the mopping up.

13 My message

In *Through Seasons of the Heart* John Powell writes, "There's an old Christian tradition that God sends each person into this world with a special message to deliver, a special song to sing for others, a special act of love to bestow.

"No one else can speak my message, can sing my song, or offer my act of love. This is my responsibility; this is entrusted to me."

– A bit frightening, isn't it? Especially if I have to answer for how I carried out my mission.

– I shall pass this way but once. Any good deed that I can do, any good word that I can say, let me do it now, let me say it now—for I shall never pass this way again.

14 Saved by prayer

Irmgard Wood was a young girl living in Germany during World War II, and she tells the following story. One morning her mother and sisters saw an American plane receive a hit, and fall in flames from the sky. Irmgard's mother instinctively whispered a prayer for the pilot, even though he was one of the "enemy."

Years later, the Wood family emigrated to America. The mother got a job in a hospital in California. One day a patient, knowing she was German, asked her what part of Germany she was from. When she said Stuttgart, he told her how he had a miraculous escape over Stuttgart during the war when his plane was hit and fell from the sky in flames.

"I got out on time, and I just don't know how I did it, because I can never remember the details. To this day I am convinced that there was somebody praying for me."

– *More miracles are worked by prayer than this world ever dreams of. It is not possible to cry out to God, and not be heard.*

– *Life is fragile —handle with prayer.*

– *Jean Vanier says that some of the greatest movements for good in the history of the world are brought about by the quiet prayers of totally unknown people.*

15 Shaped by life

So Big is a novel by Edna Ferber. In the story, a young architect named Dirk falls in love with a young artist named Dallas. Dallas admits that she likes Dirk, but she just does not love him enough to marry him. The problem she has with Dirk is that he has never had to struggle in his life, that he has always got everything handed to him.

She goes on to say that struggle is very necessary for personal growth and wholeness. It gives a person a very special kind of lovableness, and it can even be detected in a person's handshake.

– *Any compassion I have is a direct result of my own struggles and pains.*

– Any worthwhile growth in my own life has taken place during times of struggle and conflict.

– To the fool it's a problem, to the wise it's an opportunity.

16 Knowing God

An old woman was going through a time of great doubt about the existence of God. This both puzzled and troubled her because it had never happened before.

In desperation she went to a priest for help. She expected some convincing arguments to prove to her beyond all doubt that God was alive and well. She was very surprised that the priest did not take this line at all.

His advice was very simple and, at the time, didn't make much sense. He told her to go out and begin to do specific acts of love and kindness for the people in her life, and everything would be OK. She followed his advice and time proved that all doubts about God completely disappeared.

– St John tells us in his first letter: "Whoever loves knows God."

– "Those who obey God, live in him, and he in them" (1 Jn 3: 24).

17 With new eyes

Bob Evans, who was blind since birth, had an operation at the age of fifty, in which his eyesight was made functional and he could see for the first time.

His reaction was, of course, understandably extraordinary. His whole world was changed beyond belief. In a newspaper interview he shared some of his excitement, "I can't wait to get up in the morning to see what I can see. It is the most amazing thing in the world. At night I look at the stars...I'm constantly on a high. You could never know just how wonderful everything looks."

– This points to the core of a conversion, to have my eyes really opened, to see with a whole new vision.

– "Lord, that I may see..."

18 Forgiving

During the early days of the Civil Rights Movement, Montgomery, Alabama, was a real flash point. The blacks boycotted the city bus services, because of segregation. The response of the whites was to firebomb the houses of the blacks.

It was in this tense atmosphere of hatred that Martin Luther King, Jr., preached to his congregation of blacks in that same town that peace and forgiveness lay in their hands.

He went on to show them that the great act of forgiving must always begin with the person who is wronged.

– *Lord, give me the serenity to accept the things I cannot change, and that includes the people —all persons—in my life.*

19 Warts and all

This story is told about Oliver Cromwell. He was sitting for an artist who was painting a full-length picture of him.

When the painting was complete, Cromwell looked at it, and saw that the painter had gone out of his way to make Cromwell more handsome than he actually was. For example, Cromwell had warts on his face, but the painter had opted to omit these.

Cromwell would not accept the finished product. He insisted that the painter do one more portrait, only this time, he was ordered to paint Cromwell, "warts and all."

– *We don't like the "warts and all" part of who we are.*

– *We could easily prefer the painter who can make us look better than we really are.*

---

20 The poor in spirit

During the Great Depression in America, a government agency had the task of travelling through backward mountain areas, in search of poor farmers, to whom they gave some grant money for the purchase of seed, or repairing their homes.

One agent came upon an old woman living in a shack. It had no floor. Several windows were broken and covered over with tar paper. The old woman had but the basic essentials, and was just barely scratching out a living on a miserable plot of land.

The agent said to her, "If the government gave you $200, what would you do with it?" Her answer was instant: "I'd give it to the poor."

– It is a mistake for a Christian to think of money as riches.

– Many millions of good people are really rich, while having little money.

– On the other hand, I could have plenty of money, and be really poor.

21 Guilty!

A street preacher set up his soapbox on the corner of a busy section in town. He was holding forth bravely about God and our need for God, but the only response from passers-by was total indifference.

All of a sudden he switched tactics. As the office workers from a nearby building came out for their lunch, the preacher would fix an eye on one, point a long, bony finger, and shout "Guilty!" Then he would remain silent for a few seconds, select another "victim," try to catch his eye, raise his right arm, point that accusing finger, and shout "Guilty!"

The response was fascinating. In his earlier preaching, the response was a snigger, a laugh, or just nothing. Now, however,

the response was a total disquieting unease—and every one of
the office workers actually began to look guilty! It seems, the
preacher was hitting home, as if they thought he knew something about them!

– *We're as guilty as our secrets.*

– *Guilt is not from God; Satan is "the accuser of the brethren; he accuses
them day and night" (Rev 12:10).*

– *"I didn't come to condemn the world..."*

– *"Neither do I condemn you..." (Jn 8:11)*

22 Give as you receive from God

A wealthy man pondered Jesus' teaching on giving and
he was deeply depressed by the whole thing. He prayed
and prayed that he might be able to accept the teaching,
but the more he prayed, the sadder he got.

One day, when he was near despair, an angel came to comfort
him. "Why are you so sad?" the angel asked him. "I am sad," the
man replied, "because of my master's teaching on giving. Does it
mean that I have to give again and again, and again, without let-
up?" "Oh no, not at all," said the angel. "You have to give only
as long as God gives to you. If God ever stops giving to you,
then you won't have to continue to give to others. God will continue to give to you—except in much greater abundance than
you could ever give."

– *God gives me nothing for myself. He doesn't give my gift of speech to
go around talking to myself!*

– *The image of the Cross is very meaningful. What comes down from
God must go sideways to others—otherwise it stops coming. This
applies to love, forgiveness, compassion, etc.*

23 Health or wealth

One day an Indian boy found a priceless pearl. This was it! At last he was going to be rich! His days of hardship and slaving were over. He need never work again.

But when he tried to sell the pearl, his real problems began. Buyers tried to trick him, cheat him, he was attacked several times, and he soon came to believe that his life could be in danger. This came as a big shock to him. It was nothing like the "great good" he had expected. He soon came to see the pearl as a liability rather than an asset, as a burden rather than a treasure.

He had to choose between the pearl and his life of freedom. With the pearl buyers looking on, the boy went down to the beach, with the pearl—and threw it out into the sea.

– *We are often in bondage to "things"—and in the words of the song, "freedom's just another word for nothing left to lose."*

– *"Lord, by your cross and resurrection, you have set us free."*

– *Free from what? Free for what?*

– *"Having given us Christ Jesus, will the Father not surely give us everything else?" (Rom)*

– *"The one who dies with the most toys isn't the winner of the game of life" (Joseph McLelland).*

24 Bread and wine

The astronauts Aldrin and Armstrong landed on the moon on July 20, 1969. Armstrong prepared for his moon walk while Aldrin unpacked bread and wine. Aldrin describes what happened, and how he felt.

"I poured the wine into the chalice... In the one-sixth gravity of the moon, the wine curled slowly and gracefully up the side of the cup. It was interesting to think that, the very first liquid ever poured on the moon, and the very first food eaten there, were communion elements. I sensed especially strongly my unity with our church back home, and the church everywhere."

– *Bread, made from many grains of wheat. Wine, made from many bunches of grapes. Community, made from many separate persons.*

– The grains of wheat are milled,
The grapes are crushed,
The people are drawn and formed–
through information,
into formation,
into transformation.

25 When Jesus enters

A working man was strongly drawn toward a beautiful vase he saw in a stall down in the town market. He bought the vase and brought it home. The vase was so beautiful that it made his front room look drab, dull, and indeed, plain ugly. So he got bright paints, and transformed the whole room. He got colorful curtains to match the paint, a brightly patterned carpet, and he even stripped down and varnished the furniture... Because of the beauty of the vase, the whole room was totally transformed.

– When Jesus enters my heart, the areas in need of attention become, oh, so obvious.

– Holiness consists in discovering that I'm a much bigger sinner than I ever thought I was! The closer I came to God, the more obvious the contrast!

26 How real is it?

One time a group of people came to Abraham Lincoln to discuss something that had been causing some trouble. Their arguments were not based on facts but on suppositions. After listening for a while, Lincoln asked, "How many legs would a sheep have, if you called its tail a leg?" "Five" was the reply. "No," said Lincoln, "it wouldn't; it would only have four. Calling a tail a leg doesn't make it one."

– Many will call me "Lord," says Jesus, but they won't enter the kingdom of heaven (Mt 7: 21).

– If I am a Christian, I don't need to tell others—they will know it themselves.

27 The robe

There is an interesting contrast between the following two stories, each involving a robe.

The first is the story of Bartimaeus, the blind beggar in Luke 10:14-52. When Jesus called Bartimaeus to come to him, Bartimaeus stood up, took his old cloak or robe and flung it to one side, and came to Jesus. It was as if he needed to get rid of something, to let go of something, to stop hiding behind something.

The second story is Lloyd C. Douglas's novel, *The Robe*. When Marcellus, the Roman soldier, put on the robe of Jesus, which he won after they had cast lots, he experienced a deep sense of unease and disquiet. The thoughts of Jesus just won't go away. He just cannot rid himself of some deep impression made on his soul by the Galilean, and he has no peace until he becomes a Christian and joins his band of followers.

– Meeting Jesus will always mean a letting go, and a putting on, a stripping down, and a building up.

– "So get rid of the old self, which is being corrupted by its own deceitful desires ... and put on the new self, created to be like God in true righteousness and holiness" (Eph 4:22-24).

28 Good friends

Dr. Joseph Matarazzo was head of the Medical Psychology Department of the University of Oregon. He would, of course, have been in great demand as a psychotherapist, and would have contributed a great deal to the furtherance of such science.

On one occasion however, he is quoted as saying, "That more psychotherapy is accomplished between good friends over cups of coffee at ten o'clock in the morning than all day long in doctors' offices." He goes on to stress the vital importance of a good talk with a real friend, and he says that this is who is most helpful when things go wrong.

– My friend is someone who really knows me and still loves me.

– A problem shared is a problem halved.

29 Gentleness

In one of Aesop's fables there's a story about an argument between the wind and the sun as to which of them is the stronger.

To settle the argument they decide to test their respective strengths against a man who was wearing an overcoat. It was agreed that whichever of them compelled the man to take off his overcoat, that one was the stronger.

The wind began the test. It blew and blew, even to gale force, but the only reaction from the man was to wrap the coat tighter around him. The sun then took over. It didn't actually do anything. It just shone in the sky and let the heat reach the man. Within minutes the man removed his coat.

– *"Blessed are the meek for they shall possess the earth" (Mt 5:5).*

– *"You can catch more flies with a spoonful of honey than with a hundred barrels of vinegar" (St Francis de Sales).*

30 The enemy within

The Great Wall of China is one of the wonders of the world. It is said to be the only man-made structure on earth that can be seen from the moon. The cost and the effort that went into building it just boggles the mind.

When it was finished, the people relaxed. They knew they were safe. Nobody could possibly attack them now. It was impossible to either climb over or penetrate their superb protecting wall, behind which they were safe.

But their enemies got through easily. How? They simply bribed one of the gatekeepers! He opened the gate, and they came through unhindered.

– *So much for the best laid plans of mice and men!*

– *There is something of an "enemy within" in all of us, and Satan knows this only too well as he dangles temptations before the windows of our souls.*

– *If Satan's wares were not very attractive to something within me, they wouldn't be much of a temptation! Paul speaks of this in Rom 7:15-24.*

31 Do not be discouraged

A ten-year-old boy was working in a factory in Naples, before present laws on child labour were put in place. His mother was convinced that he had a good singing voice, and by working in the factory he could earn money to pay for music lessons.

His first music teacher, however, told him he did not have what it takes and it would be a waste of time and money to pursue the idea any further. The boy's mother, a poor peasant woman was not so easily put off. She encouraged her son, she told him that she believed he had talent, and she even went bare-footed, rather than buy shoes, so as to save money for his music lessons.

Her efforts bore fruit, and her son, Enrico Caruso, became one of the world's greatest tenors.

– Keep showing up (in prayer)—and don't leave before the miracle!

– The miracle happens for those who show God that they're serious about what they seek.

32 His footprints

There have been many and varied ways over the years in which people looked for signs and proofs of God's existence, and his presence in the world. One bedouin had a very simple, and for him, a very real way of being aware of God's presence.

He lived in the desert, and his own existence revolved around herding his animals—sheep, camels, or whatever. The desert around, the sky above were the floor and roof of his world. During the day he spent hours watching and herding his animals. Their footprints in the sand were his life-line to them, and made it possible for him to keep contact with, and to be always aware of their whereabouts.

He often spent hours at night looking up at the sky. The desert sky was like a book or a television scene to him. There would of course be no clouds in a desert sky, so he'd be there for hours looking up at all the action—twinkling stars, shooting, falling stars, strange unexplained lights, etc. For him, these were the footprints of God. This was the vast world of an infinite almighty God; a God, who was overlooking everything down here, a God who, through the sun by day, the moon and stars at night, was always in contact with his children. The light, like his loving care, reached right down to where each of us is.

– *"The heavens declare the glory of God, and the firmament show s forth the glory of his name" (Ps 19:1).*

– *If I want the rays of the sun to give me a tan, then I have to come out-doors, and make myself available to them… It is much the same when I pray—make myself available to his love.*

33 Making amends

The film, *The Heavenly Kid*, gives us one concept of what purgatory could be about. A young man is killed in a car crash. After his death he is faced with the task of working off the evil he committed during his life. He is given the job of returning to earth to help someone who needs assistance. The person he is assigned to help turns out to be his own teenage son, whom he fathered out of wedlock.

At one point he learns that his son is scheduled to die in a car crash, as a young man, just as he had. He is shocked, and he pleads for his son to be spared, even offering to take his son's place, and to die all over again.

This offer freed him; it was the kind of love that overcomes all sin. The man was released to go on to the fullness of life, and his son was spared the car crash.

– *"Greater love than this no one has…" (Jn 15:13).*

34 The language of love

There is a legend about an African boy called Emmanuel who was always asking questions. One day he asked the question, "What language does God speak?" No one could answer him. He travelled all over his own country with the same question, but still did not receive an answer.

Eventually, he set off in search of the answer on other continents. For a long time, he had no success. At last he came one night to a village called Bethlehem, and, as there was no room in the local inns, he went outside the village in search of a shelter for the night. He came to a cave, and he saw that it was occupied by a couple and a child.

He was about to turn away when the young mother spoke, "Welcome, Emmanuel, we've been expecting you." The boy was amazed that the woman knew his name. He was even more amazed when she went on to say, "For a long time you have been searching the world over to find out what language God speaks. Well, now your journey is over. Tonight, you can see with your own eyes what language God speaks. He speaks the language of love, that is expressed in sharing, understanding, mercy and total acceptance.'

– *"God so loved the world that he gave His only Son" (Jn 3:16).*

– *Love is…meeting another exactly as that person is.*

35 We all have something to offer

One day a little mouse was caught by a lion. The lion was ready to swallow the tiny creature, when it cried out, "Spare me, great beast! Please don't eat me. Someday I may be able to repay your kindness."

The lion, taken aback, let out a roar, threw back his head, and roared with laughter. However, he was so amused at the thought that a tiny mouse could help him, the king of the jungle, that he freed the little animal.

Sometime later, the lion was captured by hunters. He was caught in a huge net and secured to a tree, while the hunters went to fetch a truck to carry him. Along came the tiny mouse. When he saw the lion, and the predicament he was in, he began to chew at the rope. He gnawed an opening in the net, and the lion got free.

– *God can use any of us.*

– *The least significant person in my life can help set me free from my selfishness, intolerance, judgment, etc. It all depends on how I relate to them, or treat them.*

36 Faith in oneself

A Peanuts cartoon shows Charlie Brown standing all alone. Peppermint Patty passes by, and as she does, Charlie calls out to her, "Believe in me." But she keeps on going.

Next Snoopy passes by, and Charlie calls out, "Believe in me." But Snoopy just keeps on going.

Next comes Lucy—and the same thing happens.

The last picture shows Charlie sitting all alone (notice he was standing in the first picture). His head is in his hands and he is saying, "I just can't get people to believe in me."

– *I think it's reasonable to presume that, at that moment, poor Charlie didn't have too much faith in himself.*

– *Quite often when people have lost faith in themselves, they begin to have serious problem with their belief in God.*

37 Growing naturally

A boy was playing in his back garden one day, when he found a caterpillar on a bush. He had learned in school that the caterpillar becomes a butterfly, once it breaks out of the cocoon. He was a kind and helpful boy, so he thought that his good deed for the day would be to help the caterpillar on its journey. So he gently broke the shell of the cocoon and released the caterpillar. And that, simply, was the end of the caterpillar, and of any hope it had of becoming a butterfly.

– *The very struggle to break free from the cocoon is nature's way of strengthening the caterpillar. So, when the time is right, in nature's own way the new butterfly can fly away to a whole new life.*

– *The help that some people give, with all the good intentions in the world, is anything but helpful. It is in working through a process that any worthwhile growth takes place. There is a great danger in being a "fixer," and looking for instant solutions.*

38 The blind leading the blind

Before modern radio and TV became so sophisticated, a telephone operator used get a call every afternoon asking for the correct time. She was always able to give this information with great confidence. The reason for this was that she always checked her watch, and adjusted it when needed, when the whistle blew for quitting time in the local factory.

One day her watch stopped. The telephone rang, inquiring for the correct time. She explained her predicament. Her watch had stopped, and she had no way of ascertaining the correct time until the factory whistle sounded some time later.

The caller then explained his predicament. He was calling today, as he had done every other day, from that same local factory, and he had always adjusted the factory clock to agree with whatever time it was in the telephone exchange!

– *Using human means to improve or change the human condition, is like mixing water with water —I'll always end up with water!*

39 Until he comes again

The Japanese bombed Pearl Harbor in Hawaii on December 7, 1941. Soon after that they invaded and occupied the Philippines. The U.S. General Douglas McArthur was stationed in the Philippines, and on March 11, 1942, he was forced to leave the islands. Before leaving for Australia, he promised the islanders, "I shall return."

On Oct. 20 1944, two and a half years later, he kept his promise. He landed on one of the islands and announced, "I have returned."

This heralded freedom for the Philippiness.

– *"As we wait in joyful hope for the coming of our Savior, Jesus."*

– *The Christian is an eternal optimist. He knows that evil can never succeed, even if seen to be successful for a while. Jesus will return, Satan will be confined to his own kingdom of evil, the kingdom of this world will end, and the kingdom of God will be eternally established.*

40 The way to the Father

On November 26, 1965, *Time* magazine had a story that can give us all food for thought. An electrical fuse about the size of a bread box failed, resulting in 80,000 square miles along the US-Canadian border being plunged into darkness.

All the electrical power for that entire region passed through that single fuse. Without that fuse, no power could reach any point in that vast region.

– *So it is with us and God. Jesus is the door, the gate, the fuse box, and not one of us can get to the Father except through Jesus (Lk 13:24).*

– *Jesus, God's creative love, God's omnipotent almighty power—all made available down here on earth. Without him we are in total and eternal darkness.*

41 Taking leave of the body

John Quincy Adams, at 80 years of age, was shuffling along outside his home one day, when a neighbor greeted him with the question, "And how is Mr. John Quincy Adams this morning?"

The old man replied, "John Quincy Adams himself is very well, thank you. But the home he lives in is sadly dilapidated. It is tottering on its foundations. The walls are badly shaken, the roof is worn. The building trembles and shivers with every wind, and I'm afraid John Quincy Adams will have to move out of it, move on, and change residence and address before long. But he himself is very well."

– Some people carry an organ donor card around with them. It says that when the inhabitant of the body is finished with it, that others may have whatever parts they need for "repair" jobs on their own bodies.

42 A personal God

There is a story about a man who was bedridden for years. He was a deeply religious man, and prayer was his lifeline with sanity, as well as with God. After many years confined to bed, the man began to find it more than difficult to pray. This worried and depressed him greatly. It was as if God had abandoned him, as if he had lost contact with God.

One day a friend came to visit him and heard of his problem. The friend suggested something very simple. He got an empty chair, and put it by the bed. He told the man to imagine that Jesus was sitting in the chair, and he was to talk to Jesus just as he had been talking to his visitor. When the visitor left, the man in the bed began to talk to Jesus in the chair, and in no time at all he had made contact with him again. He knew that Jesus was really present with him.

– Prayer is a simple conversation between friends: I chat away, then I listen, and when I listen, he speaks.

43 Laying the foundations

It takes five years for the seed of a bamboo tree to show any growth above ground. And then it grows to a height of 90 feet in six weeks!

Five years of preparation, of putting down roots, of spreading out underground so as to have access to plenty of food. And then, and only then, does it take off.

– The five years of apparent "nothing" is like our prayer life. Unless that is deeply rooted by constant day-in-day-out time and attention, the growth appearing above ground in our lives will be as sickly and lifeless as our prayer life itself.

44 Keeping calm

It is a beautiful day in the park, and a young father is pushing his screaming child in his pram. As the father wheels his infant son along the path, he keeps murmuring, "Easy now, Donald. Just keep calm, Donald. It's all right, Donald. Just relax, Donald. It's gonna be all right, Donald."

A woman passes by and says to the young father, "You certainly know how to talk to an upset child—quietly and gently." The woman then leans over the pram and coos, "What seems to be the trouble, Donald?" and the father says, "Oh no, he's Henry. I'm Donald!"

– The best way to be in control of a situation is to take control over what's happening within me. Is it possible that there is a connection between the volume of screaming kids at Mass and the turmoil going on in the hearts of the adults present. It is an acceptable adage in educational circles that a noisy teacher makes a noisy class. What about a noisy parent?

45

As the world sees us

With a broad swipe at modern psychological testing and skill assessment, someone suggested that if Jesus had sent his twelve apostles for these tests, this might well be the reply he would have received:

"Thank you for submitting the resumes of the twelve men that you have picked for managerial positions in your new organization. All of them have taken our battery of tests. We have run the results through our own computer after having arranged personal interviews for each of them with our psychologist and vocational aptitude consultant. It is the staff opinion that most of your nominees are lacking in background, education and vocational aptitude for your enterprise. They have no team concept.

"Simon Peter is emotionally unstable and given to fits of temper. Andrew has no qualities for leadership. The two brothers, James and John, place personal interest above company loyalty. Thomas shows a skeptical attitude that would tend to undermine morale. Matthew has been blacklisted by the Jerusalem Better Business Bureau. James the son of Alphaeus, and Thaddeus definitely have radical leanings and registered a high score on the manic-depressive scale.

"One of the candidates, however, shows real potential. He is a man of ability and resourcefulness, meets people well and has contacts in high places. He is highly motivated, ambitious and responsible. We recommend Judas Iscariot as your controller and right-hand man."

– *It is his work, and it can only be done by his power. At most and at best we are only messengers, or conduit pipes.*

– *Thank God, our effectiveness as gospel people has nothing to do with our skills and talents. It is the spirit of God working in and through us.*

– *The "world" could never understand that.*

46 The light of Christ

The following story is told about John Ruskin, the 18th-century English writer, when he was quite old. He was visiting with a friend and was standing looking out the front window of the house.

It was nighttime, and the lamplighter was lighting the street lamps. From the window one could only see the lamps that were lit, and the light the lamplighter was carrying from one lamppost to the next. The lamplighter himself could not be seen.

Ruskin remarked that the lamplighter was a good example of the genuine Christian. His way was clearly marked by the lights he lit, and the lights he kept burning—even though he himself may not be known or seen.

– "... let them see your good works" (Mt 5:16).

– If we were arrested, brought to the local police station, and charged with being Christian, how many of us would get off scot-free for lack of evidence?

47 Saint

Many years ago, in less civilized times, the punishment for crime was very, very severe. One man caught stealing sheep had the letters ST (sheep stealer) branded on his forehead for all to see.

The man had a complete change of heart, and gave himself totally to God and to neighbor, and by the time he was old he was much revered and respected among his neighbors.

When the children asked their parents what the letters ST stood for, they simply said "saint."

In their eyes that was all it could possibly mean after all the years.

– A saint is a sinner who never stops trying.

– A saint is a sinner who surrendered to God, and then God took over and ran his life.

48 Appreciating life

There is a play called *Our Town*, and in it a young woman dies. As the play progresses, it happens that she is allowed by God to return to earth to re-live one day of her life. The day she chooses is her twelfth birthday.

A few hours into the day, she cries out "I can't. I can't go on. It goes so fast. We don't have time to look at one another... Oh earth, you're too beautiful for anyone to realize." Then, with tears in her eyes she asks, "Do human beings ever realize life while they live it?" A voice answers her, "No. The saints and poets maybe—they do sometimes."

– If you really want to appreciate something, have it taken away from you, and when you have lost it, have it then restored to you.

– A tragedy of life is to reach the end and realize I never really lived; I settled for existing.

– Everybody dies, but not everybody lives.

49 No coincidence

One time the hospital chaplain was told that a patient in room 101 was from his part of the country. He went to the room, only to discover it was a mistake. The person there was a total stranger to him from another part of the country entirely. The chaplain explained the mix-up, and was about to leave when the man asked him to stay. For many years he had needed and really wanted to talk to a priest, but he could never bring himself to approach one.

"Father, I've been praying for the courage to talk to a priest. I was actually praying when you walked in the door. I don't believe that you're coming here now was a coincidence. I believe it was God answering my prayer."

The man then spent the next hour unburdening himself of years of sin and of guilt, and when the priest left he was praising and thanking God for coming to him in the midst of his trouble with a terminal illness.

– It is not possible for a person to cry to God and not be heard.

– God's answers to our prayers are often so simple, obvious, and so ordinary that we may fail to believe that they come from God.

50 So much for fame

There is a story told of a singer, well known in his own locality, who was on holidays with his wife and kids in another part of the country. It was raining one of the days, so the singer, his wife, and four kids went to the movies.

When they arrived the lights were on and there were about ten people in the seats. When they entered, all ten jumped to their feet and applauded loudly. The singer was thrilled to be recognized so far from home.

A man came over and shook his hand, and the singer said, "I'm just amazed that you should recognize me so far away from home." "Recognize you?" said the man, "I haven't a clue who you are. All I know is that the manager of the cinema said he would not show the film unless six more people turned up!"

– *Sic transit gloria mundi!*

51 Why do I do what I do?

A young wife was preparing to bake a ham. Her husband was watching. He was puzzled when she took a knife and cut a piece off each end of the ham. "Why did you do that?" he asked. "I really don't know," she replied, "but my mother always did it."

Some time later the young man was visiting his wife's mother, and he remembered the incident with the ham, and his wife's explanation for doing what she did. So he asked his wife's mother why she cut a piece off each end of a ham, before baking. The reason was simple, "Because the hams sold in our local supermarket are too big for the only baking pan I have!"

– *Oh, to be reflective, to be thoughtful, and not to be afraid to stop and look at ourselves, what we do, and why we do it!*

– *On occasions I can do the right thing, but not always for the right reasons.*

– *Why I do something makes it wrong or right. I could visit someone in hospital because I feel sorry for him—or because I want to gloat over his helpless state!*

52 Love

You are all familiar with the "Love is..." cartoons or drawings. We have many, many posters of nice "sugary" definitions of love.

St Augustine answered the question: "What does love look like?" His answer is simple:

"Love has hands to help others.
It has feet to hasten to the poor and needy.
It has eyes to see misery and want.
It has ears to hear the sighs and sorrows of others.
That's what love looks like."

– The nearest I'll ever come to seeing God in this life is if I ever come across a few people who really love one another!

– Love is always creative, always building up, always confirming.

53 Salvation from Jesus

The great Lutheran pastor Dietrich Bonhoeffer was arrested, imprisoned and eventually executed by the Nazis. Shortly before Christmas 1943, he wrote a letter in which he said:

"Life in a prison cell reminds me a great deal of Advent. One waits and hopes and putters around. But in the end, what we do is of little consequence. The door is shut, and it can only be opened from the outside."

– I was carried into church one time (baptism) and I had no say in it at all. I will be carried into church one more time (funeral), and once again, I will not be consulted! Why do I think that I can manage and control all that goes on in between?

54 Lord, help me!

There is a story told about two insects, one was tiny, and the other, by comparison, was really big. The tiny insect was looking up at the large insect, and he asked, "What kind of bug are you?"

"I'm a praying mantis," came the reply. The tiny insect chuckled, and replied, "That's stupid—bugs don't pray!" With that, the mantis grabbed the tiny insect around the throat and began to squeeze. The poor little insect's eyes began to bulge. Then rolling its eyeballs heavenward, it screamed "Lord, help me!"

– *There comes a time for all of us when all we can do is cry out to God for help.*

– *When you're on your back, there's only one way to look — that's up!*

– *There are very few atheists in rubber dinghies in the middle of the Atlantic!*

55 The grain of wheat

A little boy was crying bitterly in class. The teacher asked what was wrong, and he said that his sister was really dead, because they had put her in the ground, and covered her up!

The teacher took the boy by the hand and brought him over to the window, on which was a box of clay. Some weeks earlier the class had planted seeds in the clay. The teacher explained that they were not intended to remain as seeds. They were planted in the clay, and after awhile they began to sprout and grow into plants, and flowers—which is what they were meant to become.

She poked in the clay with her finger and removed one of the seeds, which has already begun to put forth shoots, and to put down roots. "The seed is not dead," she said; "it is changing and it is now becoming what it was always meant to become."

– *"For you Christian people, life is changed, not ended."*

– *When I die, I then become all that God created me to be.*

– *If you ever wake up some morning, and you find that your life is all it should be, then, don't move —just call the undertaker.*

56 Living the gospels

Three people were discussing some recent translations of the Bible. One said, "I like the New American version. It is so much clearer than the older versions, and is so much easier to read."

The second said, "I like the Jerusalem Bible. It's not only clearer, but it's more poetic, which makes it more suitable for us in prayer."

The third said, "I like my mother's translation best of all. She translated the Bible into actions, which makes it so much easier to apply to daily life."

– You write a new page of the gospel each day
By the things that you do, and the words that you say.
People read what you write, whether faithful or true.
What is the gospel according to you?

– You may be the only gospel some people will ever read; they may never buy the books.

57 Fair is fair

This story is told about Kruger, the great South African statesman, who lived at the beginning of this century. He was called upon to settle a dispute between two brothers. The dispute involved the equal division of land between the two. The land contained mines, lakes, rivers, and beautiful scenery, and Kruger knew that no matter how he divided it, he was bound to run afoul of at least one of the brothers.

He pondered the problem at great length, and then he came up with the solution. He called the two brothers together and he gave one of them the task of dividing the land in two. When he had finished, Kruger gave the other brother his choice as to which half he wanted.

– Coming to a fair decision can often be easy; getting people to see and accept the decision as fair, can be virtually impossible.

– Have you ever been in a restaurant and ordered your meal, and were sorry you didn't order what the person at the next table had just been served?

58 Trusting the Father

A group of botanists was exploring almost inaccessible regions in search of new species of flowers. One day they spied, through binoculars, a flower of great rarity and beauty. It lay in a deep ravine, with perpendicular cliffs at both sides. To reach it, someone would have to be lowered over the sheer precipice by means of a rope, and it was certainly a very dangerous undertaking.

Approaching a young lad nearby, who was watching them with great curiosity, they said, "We'll give you twenty dollars if you'll let us lower you down below to obtain that beautiful rare flower for us." The young lad took a look away down into the ravine and replied, "Just a minute. I'll be back." When he returned he was accompanied by an older man. Approaching one of the botanists, he said, "I'll go over the cliff and get that flower for you if this man holds the rope. He's my father."

– *God sent Jesus to tell us to call him "Abba, Daddy."*

– *"I will not leave you orphans," said Jesus. Then he gave me his Father and his Mother. However, he went on to tell us that it wouldn't work unless we became like children.*

59 Reading about it

Imagine the following situation. John is six years of age. For his birthday, his father buys him a beautiful bicycle. The father, however, is a bureaucratic literalist, and with the bicycle comes a thick book, complete with diagrams, entitled, "You, too, can master the techniques of cycling." The father insists that the boy read the book, study it in great detail, memorize passages from it, and pass a written exam on its contents before he is allowed, or indeed, "qualified," to ride the bicycle!

Seems ridiculous, doesn't it? Yet we might well see people reading and studying books on prayer, for example. Or about repentance, conversion, honesty, etc.

– *I learn to pray by praying, not by reading a book about it!*

– *One of the ways in which I'll never get around to doing anything, is to read and discuss it long enough.*

60

Keeping everybody happy?

The following is a summary of the comments made about the parish priest in a typical parish:

If his homily is longer than usual: "He sends us to sleep!"

If it's short: "He hasn't bothered!"

If he raises his voice: "He is shouting!"

If he speaks normally: "You can't hear a thing!"

If he's away: "He's always on the road!"

If he's at home: "He's a stick-in-the-mud!"

If he's out visiting: "He's never at home!"

If he's in the rectory: "He never visits his people!"

If he talks finances: "He's too fond of money!"

If he doesn't: "The parish is dead!"

If he takes his time with people: "He wears everybody out!"

If he is brief: "He never listens!"

If he starts Mass on time: "His watch must be fast!"

If he starts a minute late: "He holds everybody up!"

If he is young: "He lacks experience!"

If he is old: "He ought to retire!"

And if he dies? Well, of course, "No one could ever take his place!"

– *When I die, which will God ask me to account for: the messenger or the message itself?*

– *If I don't want to hear, to listen, or to accept responsibility, then I'll always find an excuse. Some people spend their lives blaming others for everything that's wrong with themselves!*

61 The silent prayers

There is a poem called "A Legend" by Adelaide Proctor. It is about a preacher whose sermons attracted large crowds from far and near.

During all of his sermons, there was an old man in the background, who was seen to be quietly plying his rosary beads. One day the preacher was thanking God for his gift of preaching that drew so many listeners, and seemed to change so many lives.

Imagine his surprise when a voice told him that it was not his sermons that were having the great effect on people. People's hearts were being touched and changed because of the prayers of the old man who was praying his rosary beads in the background!

– *Some of the greatest movements for good in the history of the world have been brought about by the quiet prayers of totally unknown people. (Jean Vanier)*

– *For every one word I speak to people, I should have many a word with God. I go to God for the sake of people, and to people for the sake of God.*

62 As you sow

A building contractor built large luxury homes. He had no scruples whatever about cutting corners, and taking the easiest and cheapest way out of every situation.

As a result of years of experience he had become expert at this form of deception. Many of his buildings were fire hazards and danger zones, because of his shabby approach to his work.

His last house was probably his worst and most shameful attempt. But being his last house he just couldn't care, and he took all sort of risky liberties with it.

Imagine his horror when he discovered that his retirement bonus from the firm was a present of that last house he had built!

– *"As you sow, so shall you reap" (Gal 6: 7).*

– *We are often punished by our sins, rather than for them.*

– *God is eternal. Therefore God can afford to wait! The problem with us is that we get but one stab at life; we never get a second chance to go around.*

63 Seeing God

A man and his young son went on a camping trip to the mountains. They hired an experienced guide, who brought them into the heart of a great forest, and the beauty spots in the mountains that they themselves would never have found.

The old guide was forever pointing out beauty and wonders that the mere passer-by would never notice. The young son was fascinated by the ability of the guide to see so much in the surroundings.

One day the young lad was so impressed that he exclaimed, "I'll bet you can see God out here." The old guide smiled and replied, "Son, as life goes on it's getting hard for me to see anything but God out here."

– *Happy are the pure of heart they shall see God (Mt 5: 8).*

_ *God is always ready to reveal himself to those who want to see him.*

– *"I see his blood upon the rose, and in the stars the glory of his eyes..." (Joseph Mary Plunkett).*

64 Sin is here and now

A soldier had returned from the war in Vietnam. He had settled back into civilian life with his wife and kids. He was a church-going person.

One day he remarked to his wife, "Isn't it a strange thing about sin? When I was on an aircraft carrier off Vietnam, the chaplain was forever and always condemning the evils of prostitution in Vietnam—something that was far removed from where we were. Now that I'm home again, the local priest spends a lot of his time condemning the war in Vietnam."

– Only three times in the Mass am I allowed to speak in the first person singular... "I confess... that I have sinned... Lord, I am not worthy..." When it comes to sin, I must speak for myself, and stop looking so far away from home.

– Parents with kids not going to Mass: When you die you won't be asked what they did! You'll be asked what you did—did you still love them, anyhow?

65 The sign of love

A man owned a wonderful magic opal ring. The person wearing it became so good that that person was loved and respected by everyone.

The man had three sons. Before he died he gave each of the sons an opal ring. After the old man died, the three sons began to quarrel and argue among themselves about which of them had the magic ring.

They went to a wise old man to settle the dispute. "My sons," he said, "only time will show that. Your lives, how you live your lives, will show which of you has the magic ring."

– I am asked not to believe, preach, or teach the gospel—but to live it.

– If my life doesn't speak of gospel values, then there's little use in speaking about them with my tongue.

– You write a new page of the gospel each day
By the things that you do and the words that you say.
People read what you write, whether faithful or true,
What is the Gospel according to you?

– If I go into your house and tell you I have measles, when I actually have chicken-pox, which are you likely to catch?

66 The Bible

Dr. Blenton, a psychiatrist, said, to a patient's surprise, that he actually studied the Bible every day. "It is the greatest textbook on human behaviour ever put together. If enough people studied it, absorbed it, and began to live by it, most psychiatrists would be unemployed."

As an example, he spoke about the parable of the Prodigal Son, and he said that if people really believed the core of that story, namely, that God's loving forgiveness is infinitely greater than any mistake we can make, all of his patients, paralysed with guilt feelings, would walk away free and healed.

– *This Parable should be called "The Parable of the Forgiving Father."*

– *Jesus invites us to come home, where a big hug awaits—even if our faces are covered with pigs' food!*

67 Love of law

William Barclay tells the story of a rabbi who was in prison in some part of the world. It was a rigid regime, and he barely had enough food and drink to survive.

He was an Orthodox Jew who stuck to the letter of the law in everything. Each day, when he got his meager fare of food and drink, he went through all the ritual of washing before eating, using up most of his daily allowance in the process. Luckily for him he got out of the prison in time. Another short while and he would have died of thirst—all of his own making!

– *Jesus died to bring us across a bridge from a love of law to a law of love.*

– *Unfortunately some Catholics can still give more emphasis to the letter of the law, than to the spirit of love.*

68 He died for you

The body of Abraham Lincoln was lying in state. He had been murdered in Washington, D.C., and his body was being taken back to Springfield, Illinois.

The people were lined up to view the remains. In the line was a poor black woman, carrying her four-year-old son. When they reached the president's body, the woman lifted her son up in the air, and said, "Honey, take a good long look. That there man, he died for you."

– *Every mother could point to Jesus, and say those self-same words to each of their children.*

69 The power of prayer

A true story: Jim Johnson was given the job of saving a failing hotel. Others had tried, but all had failed. Jim decided to try something different.

He did all that was needed, from a materialistic and economic point of view, to make it possible for the hotel to function – but he added one extra ingredient. Every night he drove to a hill overlooking the hotel and there he prayed for one hour for God's blessing on his work in the hotel. He prayed for the staff and for the guests. He put the whole project in God's hands. At such times, he brought to God in prayer every decision he had to make. He talked to God about every aspect of running the hotel. In time, he came to think of God as the manager of the hotel, and he was just there to do God's bidding.

Very soon the situation at the hotel began to improve. There was a much more personal investment of time and interest on the part of the staff. The atmosphere became much more welcoming. The guests were really impressed, and this spread by word of mouth, and soon the hotel was doing a thriving business.

And all because one man brought the situation to God, day after day.

– *Our Lady of Medjugorje has said that we seem to have lost all concept of the power of prayer.*

– *"Prayer is one of the ways God has chosen to share infinite power with us" (Pascal).*

70 Jesus at the door

There is a story about an old monk who had prayed all his life that he might be blessed by seeing a vision. At last, one day, his prayers were answered. Just as he was beginning to "absorb" the full impact of the vision, the monastery bell rang. It was the bell which notified that there were beggars at the monastery gate waiting to be fed. On this particular day, it was this monk's turn to attend to the beggars. For a mere second he hesitated, and then, despite the attraction of the vision, he turned his back on it, and went to feed the beggars.

On this particular day there were more than the usual number, and it was over an hour later before he returned to his cell. To his surprise and delight, the vision was still there. Then Jesus, in the vision, spoke to him, and said, "Had you not gone to feed the poor, I would not have stayed."

– Jesus comes along at the most awkward moments!

– God doesn't want to hear me say "I'm sorry, I love you, praise you, thank you," unless the people around me hear it first.

71 His great mercy

A man was visiting the Holy Land. One night he found himself all alone in the garden of Gethsemane. The night was beautiful, the sky full of stars, and the whole place was still. He was deeply touched; he began to cry, as he threw himself on his knees and prayed, "Lord, don't let me ever sin again."

Suddenly a voice replied, "My son, you ask me never to let you sin again. If I granted that request to all my children, how could I ever show them my mercy?"

– Even my sins, failures and falls can be turned into good, by letting me experience God's great love and mercy, by reminding me of my own sinfulness and by developing a compassion and empathy in me for others. Who am I to throw the first stone?

72 Dying for others

A prisoner escaped from Auschwitz, a Nazi concentration camp in Poland. As a warning to the others, the prison guards picked out ten men at random, to be executed in public. One of the men was the father of a family. As the victims were being marched out to execution, another prisoner, Maximillian Kolbe, a Franciscan priest, stepped forth, and offered to take that man's place.

The officer in charge was stunned, but he accepted the offer. Maximillian died, and when he was canonised a saint some forty years later that man, whose place he had taken, was seen on international television, with tears streaming down his face.

He had met one man who really loved. "Greater love than this no man hath, that a man should lay down his life for a friend" (Jn 15:13).

– *Putting others before myself is one way to think of living a Christian life.*

73 Doing or knowing the truth

There is a story told about a guy called Hubert Courtney, who was arrested for car theft. He was a real con artist and was always ready to pull a stunt to get himself out of a jam.

To help his protestations of innocence, he stripped off his shirt, to expose a tattooed chest with the words "Crime Does Not Pay" written across it.

The judge, who was convinced of the man's guilt, remarked that the tattoos made the man even more blame-worthy, because there was such a wide gap between what he did and what he proclaimed.

– *We Christians can never say we didn't know, because God sent his own Son to tell us.*

– *Jesus says "The words that I have spoken will be your judge..." (Jn 12: 48).*

74 There is a way out

Two frogs accidently fell into a bucket of cream. They swam around and around in the cream, and every effort they made to climb up the side of the bucket was in vain. They were trapped, with no evident means of escape.

One of the frogs gave up, thinking there was no point in hoping where there was no clear hope, and he just went to the bottom and drowned. The other frog was no quitter. He was convinced that there must be a way out, and he was determined to find it. He gave it his best shot, as he splashed and thrashed around in the cream. Imagine his surprise and his relief, after a while, when he found himself sitting on top of a big lump of butter! He rested there, regained his strength, and leaped out of the bucket!

– *The only real sin for the Christian is despair. The victory is ours, but we often give up too soon, and leave before the miracle!*

– *"Always have an explanation ready to give to those who ask you the reason for the hope that you have" (1 Pt 3:15).*

75 Preparing for the journey

The king was a very smart man—sure wasn't he the king? The fool was a fool, a proper fool. The king used to laugh at the fool who said such foolish things. One day he handed the fool a staff. "Take this staff," said the king, "and keep it till you find a bigger fool than yourself."

Years past. The king was dying. His family, his courtiers, his ministers, his servants, and the fool stood around his bed. The King said, "I have called you to say goodbye to you. I am about to leave you. I go on a long journey. I will return no more to this place." The fool stepped forward. "Your majesty, one question before you go. In the past, whenever you went on a journey to far away corners of your kingdom or to some other country, you always sent heralds, police, and soldiers ahead of you to make preparations for your journey. May I ask what preparations your majesty has made for this long journey you are about to undertake?" "Alas!" replied the King, "I have made no preparations." "Then," said the fool, "take this staff, for at last I have found a bigger fool than myself."

— *"What does it profit a man if he gain the whole world and suffer the loss of his own soul?" (Lk 8:36)*

— *One day a group of people will go to a cemetery, hold a brief service, and return home. All except one—that one will be you!*

76 We are sinners

A saintly old woman was out for a short stroll one night, before going to bed. It was a beautiful night, clear sky, bright stars, full moon. The old woman was deeply touched as she looked up at the sky. With a deep sense of reverence at the awesomeness of God, and his creation, and her own limited humanity, she fell on her knees, and cried out, "O God of infinite goodness and beauty, please don't ever let me offend you in the slightest, tiniest way again." Then she heard a voice saying, "My child, if I granted that request to everyone, how could I ever show my infinite mercy and forgiveness, which is one of the clearest ways I have to let people know and experience my love?"

— *If I can forgive another often enough, I will really come to have a real love for that person.*

— *Forgiveness is the preservative that keeps love from going bad, or from dying.*

77 Let go, let God
A poem...

As children bring their broken toys with tears for us to mend,
I brought my broken dreams to God,
because he was my friend.
But then, instead of leaving him
at peace to work alone,
I hung around, and tried to help
with ways that were my own.
At last I snatched them back and cried,
"How can you be so slow?"
"My child," he said, "what could I do?
You never did let go."
— *Faith is handing something over to God, and taking my hands off it.*
— *God will not touch it until I take my hand away.*

78 We can make a difference

One day as he began his daily prayer, a holy hermit saw passing by, a cripple, a mother begging for food for her pathetically malnourished child, and the victim of what must have been a very severe beating. Seeing them, the holy man turned to God and said, "Great God! How is it that such a loving Creator can see so much suffering, and yet do nothing about it?" And deep within his heart he heard God reply, "I have done something about it. I made you."

— *Jesus ascended into heaven and took the body he had with him. Now he has no other hands but ours.*

— *To see Christ in others, and to be Christ to others—that's the ideal that the Spirit within us can make real and possible.*

79 The real me

A woman is preparing to leave home in the morning to go to work. Her job is an important one; she is in the public eye, and her appearance is something to which she must pay special attention.

She goes through her regular morning routine with great attention, and before going out the door she checks her appearance in the mirror one last time. She is satisfied with what she sees, as she remarks, "Now I'm ready to face the new day."

Just then she was very conscious of a tiny inner voice that said, "Your outer person is ready, but what about your inner person? You've had breakfast for your body, but have you nourished your soul and your spirit? Just how ready is the real you to face this new day? How much resentment, unforgiveness, guilt do you bring with you into your day—something that may well spill over on to those around you as the day goes on?"

– *How you find the people you deal with today, will be greatly influenced by what's going on within you as you leave home for work in the morning.*

– *A man has had a terrible day on the job. He comes home that evening, walks in the door, and kicks the dog lying on the carpet!*

80 Praying with faith

In one area of the country there was a severe drought, and the farm crops across the state were being ruined.

One night a mother suggested to her little daughter that she pray for rain. The little girl was in bed, and it was her night prayers. The mother was puzzled when the little girl hesitated to pray for rain.

Eventually she explained her problem to her mother. Before coming in for the night she had left two of her dolls on a bench at the back door. If the mother agreed to go out and bring the dolls indoors, then, of course, the little girl would pray for rain!

– *God never disappoints us. God always gives us the answer we're expecting!*

– *When we pray God listens to our hearts rather than our lips.*

81 Time to think

I heard of a man who got caught in a blizzard some years ago. His truck left the road, and the wheels were just spinning; there was no way he could move. It was getting dark and it seemed pointless to walk through the snow to seek help, so he decided to await the morning light before taking any action.

When he woke up in the morning his truck was completely frozen shut, and covered in snow. It was actually six days later when he was rescued from the truck. When he was rescued he was asked what he did during those long six days. He replied, with total seriousness, "I did an awful lot of thinking."

– *One wonders about the thinking and the thoughts of a person in such a situation.*

– *It is worth reflecting on how my present life would look if I had time to reflect on it for six days.*

– *One of the slogans of AA is Think, Think, Think.*

82 Listening to another

A huge truck got stuck under a bridge. It couldn't move backward or forward. Traffic was backed up for miles in either direction. An official from the company arrived, and all sorts of attempts were made to get the truck free.

A few school kids were sitting on a wall nearby, looking at all this. One little lad shouted across at the official, "Do you want to know how to get it free, mister?" "All I need now is a know-it-all, smart-ass! I don't need your advice, thank you." The young lad was unabashed as he replied, "Just let the air out of the tires and you're all right."

The man stopped in his tracks, looked at the kid and smiled—and then proceeded to let the air out of the tires! In his heart he felt that the kid had let some air out of his tires, and brought him down a bit—and he knew that he deserved it.

– Being full of himself, being a know-all, thinking of my know-how as being superior to that of those around me—that is the kind of soil in which the fruits of the Spirit can never be grown.

– Often my biggest problem is not the one I'm dealing with right then, but my inability or unwillingness to ask for help in dealing with that problem.

83 From God's viewpoint

The Eighth Day is a novel by Pulitzer prize winning author Thornton Wilder. It is about a very ordinary family. They are good and decent, but their lives are being ruined by very evil people. Wilder doesn't come down on either side as the novel ends. It is not a question of the good and innocent being seen to triumph, or of the evil being seen to suffer.

He makes one very special point, though, that does give hope. He likens the family situation to a tapestry. It is a beautiful tapestry, but, at present, the family can only see the "underside" of the tapestry, and it is impossible to appreciate it, or make any sense out of it. God, on the other hand, can see the tapestry from the other, upper, side—and to him, it is just beautiful.

– If the family could see what God can see, they would need neither faith, trust or hope—the whole potential for growth and holiness would be removed.

– No matter how ugly and unseemly everything looks, God looks through it all, to see what's in the heart, what the heart is saying.

84 Proclaiming the Word

This story is told by a missionary in New Guinea. An old man, a recent convert to Christianity, used to come to the mission hospital every day to read the gospel for the patients. One day the man was having real difficulty reading. The doctor examined his eyes, and discovered that he was going blind and would probably be totally blind in a year or two. After that, there was no sign of the man coming to the hospital. No one knew what had happened to him. Eventually a young man found him, and brought the mission doctor to him.

The old man explained to the doctor that he was busy memorizing the gospels while he still could see. "Soon I'll be back at the hospital, doctor, and I'll continue my work of teaching the gospel to the patients."

– *The barometer for my own level of being evangelized is my enthusiasm to tell the Good News to others.*

– *If I don't give away to others what God gives me, God may rightly take it away again.*

85 Gossip

A woman once went to confession and confessed that she had been gossiping about others. As her penance the priest told her to go to the market, buy an unplucked hen, and on her way back she was to pluck the hen, feather by feather, and let each feather be carried off in the wind. She did that, and returned to the priest.

He praised her for her obedience, and he said, "Now, there's one more thing to do. I want you to go back along the way, and pick up all the feathers belonging to that hen!" The woman was dumbfounded. The task was impossible. By now the wind had scattered many of those feathers miles away, out across the country. "Exactly," said the priest. "Now you see what has happened as a result of your gossiping. It is impossible to call the words back again, once you sent them on their way. Be very, very careful what you speak, and especially what you gossip. It is generally impossible to repair that damage."

– *"A great forest is set on fire by a small spark. The tongue is a small part... but it can be a world of evil" (Jas 3:5-6).*

– *If A and B are gossiping about C, usually the conversations tells more about A and B than it does about C!*

86 Judge not

A Peanuts cartoon shows Charlie Brown and Linus standing side by side. Charlie is looking at a drawing of a man that Linus has just completed.

Charlie says to Linus, "I see you've drawn the man with his hands behind his back. That shows that you're basically very insecure." "I didn't put his hands behind his back because I am insecure. I drew the man with his hands behind his back simply because I can't draw hands."

– *How often our profound insights can be so grotesquely wrong!*

87 I almost helped

A true story: A woman was standing at a intersection waiting for the light to turn green so she could walk across. As she waited, she noticed a young girl of about 17 at the other side, who was also waiting for the green light. What drew her attention to the girl was the fact that she seemed upset, in fact she was crying. Just then the lights changed. The woman kept her gaze on the young girl as they approached each other in the middle of the road. Everything in her wanted to reach out, touch her, reassure her that she cared, that nothing was beyond redemption, that she wanted to help. She hesitated, she went back from her heart up into her head, and she met and passed the girl without any communication whatever.

For the rest of that day the woman was haunted by the look of pain on the girl's face; but she was especially haunted by the fact that she did nothing.

– *I could easily end up as a "nearly" person. I nearly took the gospels seriously. I nearly lived.*

– *There's a big difference between living and existing. Everybody dies, but not everybody lives. Some people just settle for existing.*

88 Shut up, and pedal!

There is a poem that likens our relationship with Jesus to two people on a tandem bicycle:

At first, I sat in the front; Christ the rear.

I couldn't see him, but I knew he was there.

I could feel his help when the road got steep.

Then, one day, Christ changed seats with me.

Suddenly everything went topsy-turvy.

When I was in control, the ride was predictable—even boring;

But when Jesus took over, it got wild!

I could hardly hold on.

"This is madness," I cried out,
But Christ just smiled and said, "Pedal!"
And so I learned to shut up and pedal—
And trust my bike companion.

Oh there are still times when I get scared.
But Christ just smiles, touches my hand—
And says, "Pedal!"

— *Jesus says, "Follow me, let's go... stop thinking about it!"*

— *"He that follows me walks not in darkness, but has the light of life"* (Jn 8: 12).

89 The prayer that Jesus taught

In his journal, *Markings*, Dag Hammerskjold, is shown to be a prayerful person. He had a profound admiration for Jesus, and was attracted to Christianity, although he had no declared religion.

An indication of his priorities was that he was responsible for building the Meditation Room at the UN. His journal contains several references to the Lord's Prayer, indicating that it was a frequent subject or theme for his own reflection and meditation.

Here's just one brief reference from his journal, to give example of his thinking,
"Hallowed be Thy name, not mine,
Thy Kingdom come, not mine,
Thy will be done, not mine."

— *We may call it the Lord's Prayer, but are we ready to make it our prayer?*

— *The Lord's Prayer, when each phrase is reflected on and said prayerfully is itself a very powerful teaching on prayer.*

90

I or we?

A young man knocked at the door of a house. "Who is it?" said a voice from inside. "It is me," said the young man. "I've come to ask permission to marry your daughter." "You're not ready," said the voice from within, "Go away and come back in a year."

A year went by. The young man came back and knocked on the door again. "Who is it?" said the voice from inside. "It's us," said the young man. "We've come to ask your permission to marry." The voice from within said, "You're now ready. Please come in."

– *There can be a long journey from "me" to "us." Some people, when they say "we" make you wonder if they have a leprechaun in their pockets!*

– *Quite often on the wedding day, each person is happy, because "this other person meets my needs." If their marriage is really blessed, and they grow into love together, and the main concern of one are the needs of the other...now they love each other!*

91

A sin is a sin!

Anthony Mastroem wrote the following provocative comment:

No one steals any more...they simply lift something.

No one lies any more...they simply misrepresent the facts.

No one commits adultery...they simply play or fool around.

No one kills an unborn baby...they simply terminate a pregnancy.

All of this, says Maestroem, is simply a clever, if dishonest way, of candy-coating the reality of sin.

– *If God wanted a permissive society, God would have given us Ten Suggestions instead of Ten Commandments.*

– *Calling a spade "an agricultural implement" does nothing to change what it is!*

92

Forgiven and forgotten
A poem

How I wish for a wonderful place
Called the Land of Beginning Again,
Where all our mistakes,
Our sins and our aches,
Could be locked in a case
And dumped in a lake
Never to surface again.

– *God takes our sins and dumps them into the deepest lake. The problem: God puts a sign on the lake: "No fishing!"*

– *When God forgives, God suffers from total amnesia!*

– *God presses the "erase button," and the sheet comes out blank!*

93

Using the tongue

A man had a dream in which he was taken up to heaven. He was wandering around, when Jesus came along, and let him have a vision of something down here on earth. It was a church on a Sunday morning, and Mass was being celebrated. The organist was playing away, the man could see the fingers move and the keys go up and down—but he couldn't hear a sound. He could see the choir, watch them open their mouths, and sing all the words—but he couldn't hear a sound. He watched the priest and the people stand up, sit down, turn the pages of the Mass leaflets, and open their mouths to say all the prayers, but, once again, the man couldn't hear a sound.

He was puzzled, so he turned to Jesus and asked him why the silence. Jesus replied, "You see, unless these people pray or sing with their hearts, we cannot hear them here."

– *"These people honor me with their lips but their hearts are far from me"(Mt 15:8).*

– *"Loving words are on their lips but they continue their greedy ways" (Ez 33:31).*

94 Until death do us part

Ruth Youngdahl Nelson tells the following story in her book, *A Grandma's Letters to God:*

There is a huge fortress on a hill overlooking the town of Weinsberg in Germany. One day, far back in feudal times, the fortress was surrounded by the enemy. The commander of the enemy troops agreed to let all women and children leave the fortress. He also agreed to allow each woman take one valuable possession with her.

Imagine the amazement and frustration of the commander when he saw each woman leave the fortress with her husband on her back!

– *What God has joined together, let no one put asunder.*

– *When a couple get married they are but beginning a journey into love. If all goes well, then, hopefully, in about fifty years, they will have come to really love each other.*

95 God's on top of things

One day a man was walking through a field, deep in meditation and reflection. He stood in awe before a huge oak tree, reflecting on the tiny acorns lying around the base of the tree—the ones that had fallen off in the wind. He looked across the fence at a huge field of pumpkins, each one growing on a tiny vine plant. Suddenly he had a thought: "God made a mistake, surely! Why should the huge pumpkins be on tiny vines and the tiny acorns grow on a huge oak tree? It doesn't make any sense."

Just then there was a slight puff of wind and a tiny acorn fell from the oak tree, and plump! it hit him on the crown of his head. He smiled a wry smile, and said "Maybe God was on top of things, after all!"

– *God knows what's best for us.*

– *God sees farther down the road than we can.*

– *God will always do the loving thing.*

96

Whose fault?

A man came to work each day with his lunch box under his arm. At lunch time each day he went through the exact same ritual. He opened the box, unwrapped the sandwiches, took out one sandwich, separated the slices of bread, and exclaimed "Oh no! not cheese again!"

This went on every day, until, eventually his workmates could take no more. One man turned to him and said, "Look dummy, why don't you ask your wife to put something else in the sandwiches?"

"What wife? I'm not married," replied the man. "Then who makes the sandwiches?" he was asked. "I do," was the reply!

– It is a principle in computer studies that the computer can only work with the information I feed into it. Feed it junk, I'll get back junk!

– It is a sign of personal maturity to take responsibility for my life, and for the way it is.

97

He was what he thought he was

One day, Mark had a strange find. He came upon an eagle's egg, and decided to put it into the nest of a farmyard hen. In time the eaglet hatched with the hen's brood of chicks, and grew up with them.

All his life the eagle did what the farmyard chickens did, thinking he was a chicken. He scratched in the yard for worms, insects, and scraps of food; he clucked, cackled, and would thrash his wings and rise a few feet into the air.

Years passed, and the eagle grew old. One day he saw a magnificent bird far above him in the clear blue sky. He watched it glide majestically among the powerful wind currents, with scarcely a beat of its strong golden wings. The old eagle looked up in awe.

"Who's that?" he asked. "That's the eagle, the king of the birds," said his neighbor. "He belongs to the sky. We belong to the earth—we're chickens." Eventually the old eagle died a chicken. He had lived a chicken and died a chicken, for that's what he thought he was.

– *"Lord, by your cross and resurrection, you have set us free"—but how free are we?*

– *Jesus died, paid the debt and gave us his spirit, that we might be raised above and over the quicksands of our own selfishness and despair.*

– *Despite all Jesus has done, we can settle to remain in bondage, without hope, and with no way out.*

98 Incarnation

This story is told to show the difference between the teachings of Confucius and Buddha and the teaching of the gospels.

A man fell into a dark, slimy pit, and he tried to climb out, but he couldn't. Confucius came along. He saw the man in the pit, and said, "Poor fellow, if you had listened to me, you never would have fallen into that pit." And Confucius went on his way.

Buddha came along. He saw the man in the pit, and said, "Poor fellow, if he'll just come up here, I'll help him." And Buddha went on his way.

Then Jesus came along. He saw the man and said, "Poor fellow!" and jumped into the pit and lifted him out.

– *Incarnation means that God came to join us exactly where we are, as we are. God could love us from a distance, but decided not to.*

Devil's beatitudes

Blessed are those who are too tired,
busy or disorganized to meet with
fellow Christians on Sundays each week.
Their hearts are not in it.

Blessed are those who enjoy noticing
the mannerisms of clergy and choir.
Their hearts are not in it.

Blessed are those Christians who wait
to be asked and expect to be thanked.
I can use them.

Blessed are the touchy.
With a bit of luck they may even stop
going to church.
They are my missionaries.

Blessed are those who claim to love God
at the same time as hating other people.
They are mine forever.

Blessed are the trouble makers.
They shall be called my children.

Blessed are those who have no time to pray.
They are easy prey for me.

Blessed are you when you read this and
think it is about other people and
not about yourself.
I've got you.

– The devil doesn't cause me to commit sin. I'm a sinner by nature. What the devil is best at is preventing me doing the good—through my own discouragement, distractions, despair—or through the criticism and cynicism of others.

– All that is needed for evil people to succeed is that good people should do nothing.

100 Kids

"Children love luxury. They have bad manners and love to chatter. They no longer rise when elders enter the room. They contradict their parents, gobble up dainties at the table, and are tyrants over their teachers."

It's interesting to read such comments about the young. Such comments are frequently heard nowadays. What is interesting about the above comments is that they were written by a Greek philosopher 2500 years ago!

One of the differences between a man and a boy is that the man's toys are more expensive!

101 Death the leveler

This is a story about Alexander the Great told by the Greek writer Plutarch.

One day Alexander came upon Diogenes the ancient philosopher, and he was examining some bones. He had two sets of human bones in two different boxes.

When Alexander asked him what he was doing he said he was reflecting on some of the more important lessons of life. "For example," said Diogenes, "the two sets of bones here are those of your father and of one of his slaves. I have examined them now for some time, and I honestly must confess that I cannot find any difference between them!"

– I am a spiritual being who lives in a body for a while. When I die, I go on ahead, I am finished with the body (the "remains") and if I have a donor card, others can benefit from parts of my body when I'm finished with it.

– The rich man and Lazarus in the gospel (Lk 16:19-31) is another way of looking at the teaching contained in the story above.

102 The Jesus of now

This is not a story, but the lessons that can be taught from it are very crucial.

Someone said one time, "I believe in God, and I believe in Jesus, but I don't believe in the church."

– The Jesus of Nazareth and of Calvary has gone away, and now "sits at the right hand side of the Father."

– Jesus is most present in the worshipping community. That is why, in new churches, the tabernacle is less prominent. In Eucharist, the Body of Christ is nourished by the Body of Christ.

– Broken people in the church? If you ever came across the Body of Christ without the wounds, be sure it's a phony!

103 You did it to me

There is a story told, apocryphal, of course, about a black man in the south. It was pre-integration days, and he was standing outside a church that was attended by whites only.

As it happened it was quite close to where he lived, and he was seriously considering attempting to go there on a Sunday morning, rather than travel several miles to an all black church. He was standing outside, trying to get enough courage to face what would surely prove an impossible task anyhow, when he looked up, and there was Jesus standing beside him.

Jesus asked him what he was doing there, and he said he was trying to figure out a way to get into that church. Jesus smiled and said, "Oh I know well how you feel. Actually I myself have been trying for years to get into that church!"

– Religion, divorced from spirituality, can be very destructive.

– Christianity is about a person, Jesus Christ, over and above any concept of doing good, praying, etc.

104 A savior

A man dived into a raging swollen river to rescue a boy who had fallen in. It was a tough struggle. The river was in full spate, and it was a miracle of God that the man succeeded in grabbing an overhanging branch, while clinging to the boy with the other hand.

He brought the boy to safety, none the worse for his near brush with death. He brought him home, and gave him over to the care of his mother. As the man was leaving, the boy said, "Thank you very much, sir, for saving my life." The man put one hand under the boy's chin, looked him in the eye, and said, "That's OK, son! Just make sure your life was worth saving."

– We should seriously reflect on our responsibility to live a life worthy of the fact that Jesus has saved us.

– If we are saved, we should look saved, and live like people who are saved.

105 The lost page

A teacher asked her class to rewrite the Parable of the Lost Sheep in a way that would make more sense to the members of the class.

One student wrote: Suppose you had just finished typing a 100-page term paper. You had worked long hours in drafting it and typing it. You were exhausted but deeply relieved that the job was finished. You were collecting the pages to staple them and bind them when you discovered that there was one missing. Imagine the horror, the panic, the sick feeling in the pit of the stomach. You drop the other 99 pages, and begin the anxious search. Everything in you is longing and aching for a sight of that missing page. Without that page the whole project falls limp.

Suddenly, there, away in a corner, is the page. You excitedly push a chair aside, sending the 99 pages on it flying in all directions, and you are on your knees, reaching into the corner to touch and to grasp that page.

— That one page in the hand is a source of much greater joy and delight than the 99 pages scattered around the floor.

106 Amazing grace

John Newton was a slave trader in the 18th century. There was a violent storm at sea that tossed his slave ship like a matchstick. Newton was terrified, and he cried out to God, "If you stop this storm, see me safely home, I promise to cease slave-trading, and to become your slave." The ship survived, and Newton kept his promise. He became a minister of the gospel, and it was he who later wrote the hymn *Amazing Grace.*

Amazing Grace, how sweet the sound
That saved a wretch like me!
I once was lost, but now am found,
Was blind, but now I see.

— Sometimes it takes a real experience of our own helplessness to awaken us to experience God's power.

— The average person believes in God, but not everyone is aware of needing God just now.

— Someone asked one time, "If you were on the deck of the Titanic as it was going down, would you have been going around rearranging the deck chairs?"

107 With a little help from friends

Mt. Ranier is a 14,000-foot mountain in Washington State. Some years ago, nine physically handicapped people succeeded in climbing to the summit.

One had an artificial leg, five were blind, two were deaf, and one was an epileptic. In spite of all this, they climbed the mountain, and came down together, without mishap. When asked how they achieved such an extraordinary feat, one of the blind men said, "We got a lot of help from each other."

– *That must surely rank as one of the understatements of the century!*

– *A good example of the Body of Christ in action, where the blind could see with someone else's eyes, the deaf could hear with someone else's ears, etc.*

108 Getting our own back

A foolish man heard that Buddha taught that you should never return evil for evil. One day the man met Buddha, and decided to test him to see if he practised what he taught others to do. The man began to heap all kinds of verbal abuse upon the great teacher, shouting at him, and calling him all kinds of names.

All the while, Buddha listened quietly. When the man had run out of things to say, Buddha said to him "My son, if a man declines to accept a gift from another, to whom does the gift go?" "Any fool knows that," sneered the man, "The gift goes back to the giver." "My son," said Buddha, "you have just given me much verbal abuse. I decline to accept your gift." The man made no reply.

Buddha continued, "My son, a man who slanders a virtuous person is like a man who spits at the sky. The spit doesn't soil the sky: it returns to soil the face of the one who spat."

– *The "law of the echo" teaches that whether you shout, curse, sing, or laugh into an echo chamber—that's what will come back to you!*

109 Really believing

A missioner in Africa was translating John's gospel into the local dialect. He encountered many problems finding a suitable word in the dialect to fit the word used in the English translation. One such word was "to believe." There was no exact word in the dialect, so he approached one of the natives for help. When he explained his problem, the native replied that his understanding, as he listened, was that "to believe" should be translated as "to listen with the heart."

– *If my heart doesn't hear the message, the heart will not, cannot respond, and there can never be real faith. Faith is a response to love, and love belongs to the functions of the heart.*

– *Faith is in the heart, but is often practiced by the feet, by stepping out!*

110 How others see me

From 1953 to 1961 Dag Hammerskjold was U.N. Secretary General. He was on his way to a country in Africa to try to negotiate a ceasefire when he was killed in a plane crash.

When his apartment was being cleared out after his death, a personal journal was found, with an accompanying note, saying it should be published, in the event of his death. The journal was called *Markings*, and it became an overnight bestseller. The main reason for its popularity was that it was so honest and so personal. It said, in plain words, what most of us think and experience, but may never get around to putting into words.

One entry reads, "Uneasy, uneasy, uneasy—why? ...Because anxious for the good opinion of others... you have lowered yourself to wondering what will happen in the end to what you have done." Then he added, "Bless your uneasiness as a sign that there is still life in you."

– *Oh, to be free to do and say the good and not be cowed into dishonesty or insincerity, by what we fear others might think or say.*

– *There is a big difference between being narcissistic, and looking at myself in a mirror, and asking: What do you really think? What do you really want?*

111 Transfiguration

Malcolm Muggeridge and a TV crew were making a documentary on Mother Teresa. They wanted to film her and her sisters in the actual place where they worked with the dying. They had a problem. It was quite dark and it would seem natural to expect that there was insufficient light for filming. They had no proper artificial light, so they decided to proceed anyhow, dark and all as it was. To their surprise the film was just beautiful, the lighting just perfect. It was a sort of mysterious warm glow that was really, really bright.

Muggeridge, who was not a Christian at the time, was absolutely convinced that the light came from the love that was everywhere in the home. He wrote, "This love is luminous, like the haloes artists have seen, and made around the heads of saints."

– *"The holy Spirit will remind you" (Jn5:26). Our problem often is that we forget the promise of Jesus to be with us always, in all things.*

112 Body or soul

In a book called *Undergound Notes*, a Yugoslavian political prisoner describes his experiences in prison during a time of great repression in his country. He cites story after story of various prisoners he got to know during that time.

The prisoners were frequently faced with a choice: stick to your beliefs and suffer the consequences, or give in to the oppressor and avoid any physical harm.

He describes very graphically how each group fared. Those who chose to remain faithful to their consciences experienced a remarkable strength, and inner power that they never knew they had. They found they were able to face up to and come through intolerable situations. On the other hand, those who chose to save their own "skin," ended up losing everything. They lost all sense of value of life and living.

– *"For whoever wants to save his own life, will lose it; and whoever loses his life for me and for the gospel, will save it" (Mt 8:35).*

– *In less dramatic and obvious ways we are faced with this choice and this decision everyday. By our action we proclaim our believe in Jesus or we don't.*

113

Talk or action

In *My Fair Lady*, Eliza Doolittle is fed up with Freddy's letters, and his daily protestations of his love for her. His letters arrived every day, and his whole conversation was about how much he loved her. In the total frustration, she sings the song, "Show Me." In the song she says she's sick of words, of talk, of a love like the stars, etc. "If there's any love burning in your heart," she sings, "show me."

– *Love is not love until it is put into action.*

– *"Faith without good works is dead" (Jas 2:26).*

– *What you do can speak so loudly that people won't hear what you say.*

114

Scandal: wrong signals

An old man was dying, and was thought to be wondering and rambling as he talked to himself. His son listened, and eventually began to make some sense out of what he was saying. It seems he was away back when he was a boy, and he was very worried about something. The son questioned him, and eventually the source of his worry and anxiety was revealed. When he was a boy he turned the signposts around down at the local crossroads one time, and now he's really worried about how many people he may have sent in the wrong direction, how many people he may have caused to go astray.

– *This thought could easily haunt a person on a deathbed. In what way did I give scandal, or wrong values or signals to others, and in what way am I now responsible for others who may have gone astray?*

– *Jesus is the Way. He leads us back on the True Way. He is the Truth, and he is the Light. He can undo all our wrongs. He can change all things into good.*

115

Read all about it

A gifted young student graduated from an agricultural college. Full of enthusiasm he said to an elderly farmer, "I have a book that will tell you how to farm ten times better than you are doing now." After a pause the farmer said, "But I already know how to farm ten times better than I do now."

– *Quite often we know what to do, but by continuing to read books about it, it puts off the "evil day" of deciding to do something.*

– *In most cases, Jesus prefers decisions to discussions.*

– *One of the ways of never getting around to doing anything, is to keep reading about it.*

116

Turning to God

The Will-Power Problem is a book by John Sherril. In the book he describes his struggle against a certain temptation. He always opposed it, but always failed.

He sought the help of a psychiatrist, but, after a while, this, too, proved useless. Eventually he fell on his knees and cried out to God. He acknowledged his own powerlessness, and his inability to do what he knew he should do. Immediately, God came to his aid, and the temptation was removed from his life.

He realized then that he should have turned to God in the first place, and not when every other means had failed.

– *It is never a question of will power. If I have the will, God will surely give the power.*

– *I have as much chance of overcoming or removing one of my human defects or weaknesses as I have of amputating one of my limbs.*

– *When I am really willing for God to act, I will get out of the way, and let God act.*

117 Letting go

Elizabeth Brenner, in her book, *Winning by Letting Go*, describes how people in India catch monkeys.

They cut a hole in a box, and place a tasty nut in the box. The monkey comes along, puts his hand in the hole, takes hold of the nut—and then is unable to withdraw the hand with the nut in it! It seems crazy, but the monkey is caught because it just won't let go of the nut. To be free, and not be caught, all it need do is simply let go.

– *"Let go and let God" is a slogan of Alcoholics Anonymous. It means falling on my knees, surrendering to God, making a decision to stop playing God, and let God be God.*

– *Miracles happen in my life when I get out of the way, let go, and let God take over.*

118 Whose problem?

A man and his young son were traveling by train. The father unintentionally broke some minor rule, and the ticket collector flew into a rage. He scolded and berated the man at great length.

The young boy was puzzled. He couldn't understand how his father was putting up with all this abuse. He asked him why he did not retaliate, and why he chose to be silent in the face of such a tirade. The father smiled. "It's this way, son. That poor man has to put up with himself all his life. Surely it's no big deal for me to put up with him for just a few minutes."

– *In life, the miles stretch ahead of you, but the things that trip you up in life are inside you.*

– *The day I feel good about me, I think you're OK too! And the day I don't feel good about me, then God help you!*

– *The person who hates himself or herself shows this by not having a good word to say about anybody else.*

119 For or against

It was during the Mexican War. Thoreau, the philosopher and writer, vehemently opposed to the war, because he believed it to be an attempt to expand slave-holding territories. He refused to pay taxes, because the money was going to the war effort. He ended up in jail, rather than pay taxes.

Emerson, another philosopher and writer, a friend of his, and someone who was also strongly opposed to the war and to slavery, visited him in prison.

Emerson asked Thoreau, "Henry, why are you in prison?" Thoreau looked him straight in the eye, and quickly asked him, "Waldo, why are you not here?"

– Happy are they who dream dreams, and are prepared to pay the price to make their dreams come true.

– The acid test of our conviction about anything is our willingness to be faithful to it, no matter what the consequences.

120 The least of these

A king who had no son to succeed him posted a notice inviting young men to come along and apply for adoption into his family. The two qualifications were love of God, and love of neighbor.

A poor peasant boy was tempted to apply, but felt unable to do so because of the rags he wore. He worked hard, earned some money, bought some new clothes, and headed off to try his luck at being adopted into the king's family.

He was halfway there, however, when he met a poor beggar on the road, who was shivering with the cold. The young man felt sorry for him and he exchanged clothes with him. There was hardly much point in going any further toward the king's palace at this stage, now that he was back in rags again. However, the young man felt that, having come this far, he might as well finish the journey.

He arrived at the palace, and despite the sneers and jibes of the courtiers, he was finally admitted into the presence of the king. Imagine his amazement to see that the king was the old beggarman he had met on the road, and he was actually wearing the good clothes the young man had given him! The king got down from his throne, embraced the young man, and said, "Welcome, my son!"

– There is a direct lesson in this story to show the welcome of God for the kind and the good when they come before him after death.

– "Whatever you do to the least of these, that's what you do unto me" (Mt 25:40).

121 Good or bad?

In Carl Sandburg's poems there is one called *The Muckers*. It was the time of the Depression when work was scarce and money was scarcer. A crew of workmen were digging a ditch for a pipeline. The job was both dangerous and dirty. At times, the men were knee deep in mud.

Up above them is another group of men, looking on. They are unemployed, and unable to find work. The men in the trenches say, "What an awful filthy job to be doing!" The men looking on are aware of not a little envy, as they say, "I wish I had that job."

– To the fool every opportunity is a problem, but to the wise every problem is an opportunity.

122

Follow me

Some years ago there was a plane crash in an African jungle, and the only survivors were three European businessmen and a young African boy. The boy offered to lead the men out of the jungle to safety, but, scornful of his youth, and trusting their superior "experience," they chose to find their own way. The boy reached safety, and when a search party went in search of the three men they found their dead bodies in the thickest part of the jungle.

– *"Come, follow me" presumes humility on my part to respond.*

– *It also presumes an honest admission that I am lost, and cannot possibly find my way home by myself.*

– *Acknowledging my urgent need for a savior is the basic requirement for salvation.*

123

Jesus, yesterday, today, and forever

Arnold Toynbee worked for many, many years on his monumental history of the world. The mind boggles at the vastness of the task. Near the end of this epic endeavor, he wrote one highly significant paragraph:

"When we began this work, we found ourselves looking at a great parade of marchers. But as it passed, the marchers all fell, one by one, by the wayside. And now, only one marcher remains, growing larger and larger with each step."

– *The marcher is Jesus Christ.*

– *It must be the certain hope of a Christian that the Stalins, the Hitlers of this world may stride the stage for a while, and then be no more.*

124 Perseverance

Wilma Rudolph was a disaster from birth. She was a tiny premature baby, who caught pneumonia, then scarlet fever, and finally polio. The polio left one leg badly crippled, with her foot twisted inward.

Until the age of eleven, Wilma hobbled around on metal braces. Then she asked her sister to keep watch while she practiced walking without the braces. She kept this up every day, afraid that her parents might discover what she was doing and she might be compelled to stop. Eventually, feeling guilty she told her doctor, who was flabbergasted. However he gave her permission to continue as she was, but only for a short period of time.

Anyhow, to make a long story short, Wilma worked away at it until she eventually threw away her crutches for good. She progressed to running, and by the time she was sixteen she won a bronze medal in a relay race in the Melbourne Olympics. Four years later, in the Rome Olympics, she became the first woman in history to win three gold medals in track and field.

She returned to a ticker tape welcome in the U.S., had a private meeting with President Kennedy, and received the Sullivan Award as the nation's top amateur athlete.

– *We can grow in faith, love, patience, etc, by day-in-day-out practice and perseverance.*

125

Example speaks loudest

Some young Christians were attending an international summer camp. One of the projects set before them was to discuss and explore ideas for spreading the gospel in the world.

The discussion was wide and varied. It included the use of television and radio programmes, newspaper articles, notices in magazines, and so on. Finally, when they were out of ideas, an African girl stood up and gave her opinion:

"In my country, when we think that a pagan village is ready for Christianity, we don't send them books and missionaries. We send them a good Christian family. The family's example is a more powerful proclamation of the gospel than all the books in the world."

– *"You shall be my witnesses," says Jesus (Acts1:8).*

– *"By this shall men know that you are my disciples, if you love one another" Jn 13:35).*

– *The witness value of Christianity is central. A Christian is in the business of attracting, not promoting.*

126

What is your treasure?

The New York Times carried a story, some years ago, about a 90-year-old widow, who was found, close to starvation, in a run-down, rat infested apartment. She had been well known in the neighborhood as someone who was always to be seen rummaging in garbage cans for scraps, or collecting cardboard and bits of sticks for the miserly fire she occasionally lit in the winter. She lived on hot dogs.

Three weeks later, the woman died in a New York hospital. When they cleaned her apartment they found $275,000 in paper money stashed away in cardboard boxes.

– *This woman had a lot of money, but she was really very, very poor.*

– *It is the paradox of the gospel: What I give away in life takes on an eternal value, is invested in the vaults of heaven.*

– *What I keep for myself, and don't share—when I die, it dies too.*

127 Loaves and fishes

A middle-aged woman walked into the slums of a large city. She had two dollars in her purse, had no income, and no place to stay. All she had was a deep conviction that God was calling her to doing something for the poor in that area. And she felt certain that, if the call was really from God, that he would provide all that was needed.

That woman was Mother Teresa. Today, she is known and respected the world over. She has 80 schools, 70 leprosy clinics, 30 homes for the dying, and 40,000 workers and co-workers the world over. She had nothing to start with but the equivalent of a few loaves and fishes, but she made them available to God, and many thousands continue to be nourished and cared for. She has, indeed, done something beautiful for God.

– *It is not what we have, by way of gift, talent, accomplishment. It's what we make available for God to use.*

– *Mary didn't do anything; she let God do whatever God chose with her and through her.*

– *God needs my permission before he can do anything for me, or with me.*

128 Sobriety

An alcoholic fell on his knees and cried out to God for help. God heard his cry, and in quite an extraordinary way he touched the man's heart, and led him out of the bondage of his addiction. This was a dramatic spiritual experience for the man, who felt as if he had been born again. In the workplace he spoke of this extraordinary intervention of God, and how he had now turned his will and his life over to the care of Jesus. One man scoffed, "Don't tell me you have started to believe all that rubbish about miracles, about turning water into wine, for example." "Well now," said the man, "speaking of miracles, in my house God has actually turned wine into food."

– *Miracles begin when I stop playing God, and God is free to take over, and be God!*

– *It is not possible for a person to fall on his knees, cry out to God, and not be heard.*

129 God within

An old man and his little granddaughter were at a deep well on the farm, and the man was drawing out water for the animals. He lowered the bucket into the well, and poured the water into a barrel nearby.

The little girl was playing around, looking up into the clear blue sky, and then peering down into the deep well.

Suddenly, with the spontaneity of a child, she asked, "Grand-dad, where does God live?" The grandfather lifted her in his arms, held her out over the clear deep waters of the well, and asked her, "What do you see when you look down there?" "I see myself," said the girl. "And there," said the grandfather, "is where God lives—in you."

– *"Surely you know that you are God's temple, and that God's Spirit lives in you" (1 Cor 3:16).*

– *The surest place to find God is in the temple of our own hearts. Would that this could become a Prayer Room, rather than a Pity Parlor!*

130 Radio or television

Fulton Sheen used to compare the Old Testament to radio, and the New Testament to television. In the Old Testament, you could hear the word of God, but in the New Testament, it was the word of God in living color!

This is a gigantic step forward. "He who sees me, sees the Father," says Jesus (Jn 14: 9). Jesus came "to do and teach" (Acts 1: 1). He showed us what to do by what he himself did, and then he taught us what to do.

– *"I have shown you by my example... you now do as I have done" Jn 13:15).*

– *It is very important to believe and to know that Jesus is the fullness of God's revelations—there's nothing more we need to know.*

– *Some people listen to Jesus, but imagine there's another God "up there somewhere"—usually with a notebook and a long white beard— and God is not to be trusted at all!*

131 To love his son

A wealthy man lost his wife when his only child was very young. A housekeeper came to work in the house, and to take care of the boy. The boy died tragically at twenty years of age. The old man was without kith or kin, and he died of a broken heart some years later.

He had no heir to his enormous estate, nor could one be found. Neither was there a will, so the whole property passed to the state. In due course there was an auction to dispose of the personal effects of the mansion.

The old housekeeper attended the auction, not because she could buy anything but her grief was too strong to keep her away. There was only one thing in the whole collection that attracted her attention. It was a photo of the son. She had loved him as her own. No one wanted the photo, and her few pence were enough to buy it.

She brought it home, and proceeded to take it from the frame. When she opened the back of the frame some papers fell out. They looked important, so she brought them to a lawyer.

The lawyer looked at her and laughed saying, "You sure have landed on your feet this time. The old gentleman has left all his estates and all his money to the person who loved his son enough to buy the picture."

– Jesus has told us that if we love him, the Father will love us (Jn 14: 21).

132 To walk with God

The following lines speak for themselves:

I got up early one morning
And rushed right into the day;
I had so much to accomplish
That I didn't have time to pray.

Problems just tumbled about me,
And heavier came each task.
"Why doesn't God help me?" I wondered.
He answered, "Because you didn't ask."

I wanted to see joy and beauty,
But the day toiled on, grey and bleak.
I wondered, "Why didn't God show me?"
He said, "Because you didn't seek."

I tried to come into God's presence;
I used all my keys at the lock.
God gently and lovingly chided,
"My child, you didn't knock."

I woke up early this morning,
And paused before entering the day.
I had so much to accomplish,
That I had to take time to pray!

Author unknown

— *The ideal: John gets out of bed in the morning, goes on his knees, thanks God for the gift of today. He then hands the day back to God, asking God to take it and care for it, and to be with John, and all he does or says throughout the day.*

— *At nighttime, John goes on his knees again and says, "Thank you."*

- *And any time during the day, when John got anxious, afraid, flustered, worried, etc, he knew that that meant he was taking that part of the day back from God, and was holding himself responsible for it.*

133 The evidence of baptism

This story is told by a missionary who spent many years working with primitive people. He was particularly puzzled by one man who simply refused to be baptized. At first, the man refused to give a reason. Later on, however, he explained why he was holding out against being baptized. It seems some of his friends had agreed to be baptized, so he decided that he would hold back, and watch carefully to see if baptism made any significant difference in their lives. After a year or two he came to the missioner and announced his willingness and his desire to be baptized.

– *The witness value of Christianity is very important. "You'll be my witnesses," says Jesus, "to the ends of earth" (Acts 1:8).*

– *If my life is not proclaiming the message of the gospel, then my words never will.*

– *Christianity is much more about attracting than promoting.*

134 The Spirit in the words

One time Mother Teresa of Calcutta was interviewed by Malcolm Muggeridge for a television program. The result was less than satisfactory, and the producers were not convinced that it should be screened. Mother Teresa's accent was indistinctive, and her delivery was halting.

The program, however, was shown and there was an overwhelmingly positive response to it from all over the country. There was a power in the words that comes from the Spirit. The listeners were profoundly touched by the words they heard.

– *My words alone will never hurt or help anyone; it is the Spirit in the words that hurts or helps.*

– *I should always ask and trust the Spirit of God to be in the word I speak or write, so that the words will reach the heart of the hearer or reader.*

– *Lord, may your Spirit within me touch the hearts of those I meet today, either through the words I say, the prayers I pray, the life I live, or the very person that I am.*

135 Sharing our food

There is a legend told about Abraham in the Mideast. According to the legend, he always held off eating his breakfast each morning until a hungry person came along to share it with him.

One day an old man came along, and of course Abraham invited him to share his breakfast with him. However, when Abraham heard the old man say a pagan blessing over his food, he jumped up, and ordered the man from the table, and from his house.

Almost immediately, God spoke to Abraham. "Abraham! Abraham! I have been supplying that unbeliever with food every day for the past eighty years. Could you not have tolerated him for just one meal?"

– *There is a saying about sharing our food with strangers, and unknown to ourselves, actually entertaining angels.*

– *Even a cup of cold water, shared with another, will not go unrewarded (Mt 10:42).*

– *Jesus has strong words to say about those who only love or share with those who are friends, or with those who can give in return (Mt 5:47).*

136 He took my place

A missionary in India was showing slides of art that depicted events in the life of Jesus. It seems the slides were excellent, of clear quality, and almost photographic.

Anyhow, the small group of people watching the slides were completely absorbed in their reflection on the events being shown. When the slide of Jesus on the Cross was shown, one old man ran up to the screen, and shouted, "Come down from the cross, Jesus, Son of God. I'm the one who should be hanging there, not you."

– *When I really believe, I have begun to get to the heart of Calvary and its mystery.*

137
Saint or sinner?

This story is told about Leonardo da Vinci, when he was painting "The Lord's Supper." He chose an attractive young man called Pietri Bandinelli to be his model for Jesus in the painting.

The complete work took several years to finish. The final character was Judas, and Leonardo went into the slums, and all of the "dives" in town looking for someone who would serve as a model for Judas. He was looking for someone who would clearly stand out as such in any gathering.

He found the perfect man, one who was depraved and vicious looking. Later as he was painting, Leonardo sensed there was something familiar about the man, and he asked him if they had ever met before. "Yes, we have," replied the man, "but much has happened in my life since then." He said his name was Bandinelli, that it was he who was the model for Jesus some time before.

– *It is important, more important, to remember that the reverse could equally be true—the Judas of yesterday could be the Jesus of today.*

– *After all, a saint is a sinner whom Jesus saved and sanctified.*

138
Showing the way

A man had a dream, in which he was looking at his teenage son walking along a road. The boy was strolling, skipping, and trotting along the road, without a care in the world. Suddenly, without warning, the boy turned off into a narrow dark laneway to the left, and as he moved further away, he turned to his dad and said, "You never did show me the right path to follow, anyhow."

The father woke up with a shock, and it was some seconds before he realized it was just a dream. However, it had a profound effect on him. Showing the correct path to his children had now become a priority with him.

– *Parents are like sign posts, in a way; they can point the way, but they cannot compel anyone to travel down that way.*

– *When I die, I will be asked what way I pointed, not which way the other chose to travel!*

139 The truth

This is a scene with which many hitchhikers are quite familiar. The motorist comes along the road, and suddenly is confronted with the hitchhiker with the thumb in the air, or the notice held out.

What is the motorist to do? Just keep going, or stop to give the hiker a lift? What do some of them do? The indicator of the car comes on to show that he is turning right or left—and then when safely past the hiker, the indicator is switched off, and he continues down the road.

– *There are so many, many ways of telling a lie.*

– *The hitchhiker, or at least one to whom I spoke, would much prefer if the motorist stopped and said "No"!*

– *"Let your yes be yes and your no be no!" (Mt 5:37).*

140 God's love

An anonymous poet wrote:

Could we with ink the ocean fill,
And were the heavens of parchment made;
Were every stalk on earth a quill,
And every man a scribe by trade;
To write the love of God above,
Would drain the ocean dry.
Nor could the scroll contain the whole
Though stretched from sky to sky.

– *I asked how much God loved me, and God stretched both arms fully sideways, and said "This much"—and then he died.*

141 Gossiping

Three priests were on a retreat together. They were sharing their struggle and difficulties with each other. The atmosphere seemed right, and it seemed safe to share at a depth that was much deeper than usual.

One priest confessed to being a secret drinker, and he gave much detail of how he managed to conceal and cover up that fact. The second priest confessed to having a gambling addiction, even to using money from the parish account to feed his addiction. He spoke of his dread of the inevitable when he could no longer cover up, and his scam would be uncovered.

The third priest was reluctant to share and it was only after persuasion that he confessed his secret weakness: he was an incurable gossip. He has never been able to keep a secret!

– *"If anyone can contain his tongue, it proves that he has perfect control over himself in every other way" (Jas 3:2).*

– *I may not plant a bomb or fire a bullet, but I can destroy others with a word.*

142 To complete his work

Puccini wrote *La Bohème* and *Madame Butterfly*. It was during his battle with terminal cancer in 1922 that he began to write *Turandoe*, which many now consider his best.

He worked on the score, day and night, despite his friends advice to rest, and to save his energy. When his sickness worsened, Puccini said to his disciples, "If I don't finish *Turandoe*, I want you to finish it." He died in 1924, leaving the work unfinished.

His disciples gathered all that was written of *Turandoe*, studied it in great detail, and then proceeded to write the remainder of the opera.

The world premier was performed in the La Scala Opera House in Milan in 1926, and it was conducted by Toscanini, Puccini's favorite student. The opera went beautifully until Toscanini came to the end of the part written personally by Puccini. He stopped the music, put down the baton, turned to the audience, and announced, "Thus far the master wrote, but he died."

There was a long pause; no one moved. Then Toscanini picked up the baton, turned to the audience, and, with tears in his eyes, announced, "But his disciples finished his work." The opera closed to thunderous applause, and to a permanent place in the annals of great works.

– *"He sent the Holy Spirit to complete his work on earth" Euchristic Prayer IV).*

– *Jesus has won the war, he has claimed and proclaimed the victory. It only needs us poor foot soldiers to mop up, and to announce the victory.*

143 Why no change?

Mike was a Christian, and his pal Joe, an atheist. Joe lost no opportunity to have a "go" at Mike about what he saw as the irrelevance of Christianity.

One day they were out for a walk when they came across a gang of "toughies," who were fighting and swearing. Joe pointed to the scene, and said, "Look, Mike, it's been 2000 years since Jesus came into the world, and it's still filled with aggression and violence." Mike said nothing.

Five minutes later they came upon a group of dirty faced children. Now it was Mike's turn. He pointed to the kids and said to Joe, "Look, Joe, it's over 2000 years since soap was first discovered, and yet the world's still filled with dirty faces."

– *Nothing happens until you use the soap!*

– *There is nothing automatic about Jesus or his message. It's like discovering a cure for cancer. Nothing happens until the patient takes the medicine.*

144

Are you Jesus?

One day a religion teacher began a class on Jesus by saying to some young children:

"Today I must tell you about someone whom you all must meet. He's a person who loves you and cares for you, even more than your own family and friends. He's a person who's kinder than the kindest person you know. He's a person who forgives you, no matter how often you do wrong. No matter what you do wrong, he is always ready to accept you, to love you, and to understand."

The teacher noticed a little boy getting more and more excited as he talked. Suddenly the little boy could hold back no longer. He blurted out, "I know the man you're talking about. He lives on our street."

– *To be a Christian is to be someone who shows others, in practice, some of what Jesus is like.*

– *It is important to Jesus that others recognize us as belonging to him: "By this will all men know that you are my disciples, if you have love one for another" (Jn 13:35).*

– *"You shall be my witnesses...to the ends of the earth" (Acts 1:8).*

145

Looking for an escape hatch

There is a story told of W.C. Fields, the comedian. He had reached the top rung of his profession, was wealthy, and very successful. Even to this day, other comedians specialize in mimicking him.

But his lifestyle was often seen to be at variance with gospel living. Toward the end of his life, however, he spent a lot of time reading the Bible. Someone asked him why he did this, and he replied, "I'm looking for any loopholes I can find!"

I have known one or two such people who, when the end approached, left a considerable sum of money to have Masses said for them after they died. Would it be too cynical to refer to this money as some sort of fire insurance—for the next life?

– *The road to heaven is heaven, and I am free to choose to travel that road now. It's not that simple to skip from one road to another. It is a total gift, and presumes a very special attitude of heart in me.*

146 Changed residence

This story is told about a pastor of a small congregation. He kept a meticulous register of all his parishioners. So convinced was he of life after death, and of the promises of Jesus about eternal life, that, whenever a parishioner died, he did not delete the name from the register. He simply wrote after the person's name, "Changed residence. Gone to live elsewhere!"

Those belonging to us who have died have not gone away, they have simply gone ahead.

– There is the womb life, the womb of life, and the fullness of life. It is only when a person has reached that third state that he/she has become what he/she was created to be..

147 Judging!

One day a partially deaf lad was given a note from his teacher to give his mother, suggesting that she take him out of school, because he was too stupid to learn.

The mother's reaction was to set to it, and begin teaching him herself. The boy grew up, and Thomas Edison, for that was his name, left a wealth of inventions that leaves us all deeply in his debt.

He invented the motion picture, the record player, and the light bulb. When he died, the U.S. as a nation switched off all electric lights for one minute in his memory, at a time decided on at the national level.

– How wrong we can be in our judgments!

– Herb Barks wrote: "God don't make no junk!" How often do people find themselves on the scrapheaps of life through the rejection of others?

148 The Good Shepherd

Two flocks of sheep shared the same pen at night. Early in the morning, one of the shepherds opened the pen, and cried out "Marah," which is the Arabic for "follow me," and all of his sheep left the pen and followed him.

Another man, watching this, was fascinated so he borrowed the other shepherd's cloak and staff, and cried out "Marah"—and none of the sheep paid the slightest heed to him! He asked the shepherd if any of the sheep would ever follow someone else rather than him. "Yes," said the shepherd, "sometimes a sheep can be so sick that it will follow anyone!"

– *"I am the Good Shepherd; I know mine, and mine know me. They will heed my voice."*

– *Seldom have I seen a young person get into trouble without having being led there by someone else. Surely we must accept that the opposite is always true. Therefore, we all have an obligation to give leadership.*

149 Out of the body

Two soldiers were taking part in a battle. On several occasions before going into battle, they had talked about death, whether each had a soul, what happens when one dies, etc. In the heat of the battle, a shell landed right where they were, and one of the soldiers was killed instantly. Miraculously, the other escaped unharmed.

He looked at his dead friend, or rather the corpse of his friend, and all doubt about the existence of the soul left him. This was not his friend; it was but an empty, spent shell. Everything that he loved about his friend had gone—his charm, personality, intellect, spirit had gone. What was left was nothing at all, a pitiful thing.

As he continued to look and to reflect, it was obvious to him that his friend had obviously left his shell, had separated from it, and what was left should be disposed of, either through cremation or burial.

– *I will never go into a coffin…my body will.*

– *I can have a donor card for any parts of the body that are still useful after I have finished with them!*

150 A bundle of possibilities

William Barclay tells the story about an old school teacher. Before beginning to teach a class, he used to stand before his class and bow to them. He always did this with great reverence.

One day, someone asked him why he did this. He replied that he did this because he just didn't know how any of the children might turn out. He saw each child as a bundle of possibilities, and he bowed in the belief that many of them would become unique, special, and worthy of deep respect in later life.

God endows each of us with the potential to become great, in the best sense of that word.

– *Others deserve respect, have a right to it; it is what a human being should receive. Quite often it comes only when the other has merited it through success, authority, power or influence.*

– *Everybody is on earth with equal right. The most handicapped child is on this earth with as much right as the greatest genius that ever lived.*

Of Related Interest...

Homilies Alive
Creating Homilies that Hit Home
Msgr. Francis P. Friedl & Ed Macauley
A very practical book that defines, explains and exemplifies 10 fundamentals
that will make homilies come alive for congregations.

ISBN: 0-89622-574-7, 144 pp, $9.95

More Telling Stories, Compelling Stories
William J. Bausch
While capturing the essence of the lectionary readings, Fr. Bausch makes them
relevant to the Christian assembly today.

ISBN: 0-89622-543-8, 176 pp, $9.95

Timely Homilies
The Wit and Wisdom of an Ordinary Pastor
William J. Bausch
Here Fr. Bausch uses specific gospel readings as springboards for comments on
current topics and events that both teach and delight.

ISBN: 0-89622-426-0, 176 pp, $9.95

Telling Stories, Compelling Stories
35 Stories of People of Grace
William J. Bausch
The gospels are illuminated with examples of people from the past and present
living fully as Christians.

ISBN: 0-89622-456-2, 192 pp, $9.95

Windows on the Gospel
Stories and Reflections
Flor McCarthy
The riches of the gospels are revealed through stories and reflections.

ISBN: 0-89622-545-3, 176 pp, $9.95

Available at religious bookstores or from

TWENTY-THIRD PUBLICATIONS
P.O. Box 180 • Mystic, CT 06355
1-800-321-0411